A VIEW FROM THE TOP

A VIEW FROM THE TOP

MOVING FROM
SUCCESS TO SIGNIFICANCE

ZIG ZIGLAR

Published and distributed by:

SOUND WISDOM
P.O. Box 310
Shippensburg, PA 17257-0310

717-530-2122

info@soundwisdom.com

www.soundwisdom.com

While efforts have been made to verify information contained in this publication, neither the author nor the publisher assumes any responsibility for errors, inaccuracies, or omissions. While this publication is chock-full of useful, practical information, it is not intended to be legal or accounting advice. All readers are advised to seek competent lawyers and accountants to follow laws and regulations that may apply to specific situations. The reader of this publication assumes responsibility for the use of the information. The author and publisher assume no responsibility or liability whatsoever on the behalf of the reader of this publication.

Cover/jacket designer: Eileen Rockwell

ISBN 13 TP: 978-1-64095-100-6

ISBN 13 eBook: 978-1-64095-095-5

HC ISBN: 978-1-64095-094-8

For Worldwide Distribution, Printed in the U.S.A.

1 2 3 4 5 6 7 8 / 23 22 21 20 19

CONTENTS

INTRODUCTION

ZIG ZIGLAR dedicated his life to teaching people to be part of successful living. Countless individuals attribute their success in life to having heard Zig either at one of his supercharged seminars or one of his exciting audio programs.

Yet despite the incredible impact Zig had on others, he himself realized that being successful is only part of life's challenges. He discovered that financial or career success very often can be short-lived. Many times people are left with the feeling of dissatisfaction. They arrive at their goals in life and discover that though they possess many of the things that money will buy, they lack the important aspects of life that money won't buy.

Success is worth the time and effort, but it's not enough to sustain a lifetime at the top. After success, the next step is to move from success to significance. *A View from the Top* is an exciting chapter in Zig Ziglar's personal journey of self-discovery.

Zig shares with you his most intimate discoveries as to what he personally found to be the most important elements of a truly significant life. Drawing on more than forty years as a world-class motivational speaker, Zig identifies and shows precisely how to achieve what people want most from life—to be happy, healthy, reasonably prosperous, secure, to have friends, peace of mind, a firm spiritual foundation, good family relationships, and most important—hope. As Zig delves into the hows and whys of living life with values, character, honesty, integrity, and sensitivity, you'll learn to be more at peace with yourself, accomplish more with your skills and abilities, and tap into what life is really all about.

A View from the Top will persuade you to commit to being the best you can be and convince you to recognize and continue to develop what you already have, what you can and will do. Zig will also teach you:

- How to bring the spiritual dimension to all areas of your life.

- The power in giving others a hand up not just a hand out.

- How to make radical changes in your life beginning with small steps.

- That character *does* count.

- How to combine your mission and your vision.

- The secret to following through and finishing well.

INTRODUCTION

Whether you have followed Zig Ziglar for many years or are experiencing him for the first time, this book will be a life-changing experience for you. The lessons will help you achieve success and significance; and when that happens, you reach the top and find that the view from there is simply magnificent.

CHAPTER 1

SUCCESSFUL LIVING

You're at the top when you're mature enough to delay gratification and shift your focus from your rights to your responsibilities—when you know that failure to stand for what is morally right is a prelude to being the victim of what is criminally wrong.

This is an exciting day! You are going to learn how successful living begins with a view from the top. I'm going to start your journey to the top by asking you four questions:

1. Is there something you can specifically do in the next three weeks that you know for sure, without a shadow of a doubt, would make your personal life, your family life, and your business life worse?

2. Do you honestly believe there's something you can do in the next three weeks that will make your personal life, your family life, and your business life *better?*

3. Do you believe those choices are yours to make?

4. Do you believe every choice has an end result?

You might not realize it, but let me tell you what you just agreed to. You just in essence said, "Look, I'm not really concerned about what happened in my past. I'm not even overly concerned about where my situation is and what my situation is right now because there's something I can specifically do right now that will make my future either better or worse. And the choice is mine." That's profound! That statement says that you are not a victim.

GOOD DECISIONS REAP GOOD BENEFITS

I'm calling on you, beginning right now, to start making decisions that will give you immediate benefits—infinitely more important benefits. Benefits to you now and down the road five years from now, ten years from now, even one hundred years from now, decisions that will make a huge difference to others as well. Psychiatrist Smiley Blanton said that in all his years of practice, he never knew a senile person, regardless of age, who did these three things:

- Number one, they stayed active physically;

- Number two, they continued to grow mentally and learn things;

- And number three, they had a genuine interest and concern for and about other people.

In other words, healthy people are not self-centered individuals.

I regularly meet people who are not focusing on what is important. We need to keep the main thing the main thing if we're going to accomplish the main objectives. Social philosopher Eric Hoffer said that in times of change the learners shall inherit the earth while they learn. The learned find themselves beautifully equipped to deal with a world that no longer exists. And how true that is. We've got to be ever learning.

> **HEALTHY PEOPLE ARE NOT SELF-CENTERED INDIVIDUALS.**

My friend and mentor Fred Smith said that he has a right not to have a degree, but he also doesn't have a right not to have an education. And I could not agree more. Fred never went to college except to teach and accept a lecture and accept a counsel. But Fred was right. My administrative assistant for the past twenty-four years finished tenth grade. About seven or eight years ago, we evaluated our key personnel. She checked out at slightly above the Master's degree level. Now she did not move from tenth grade to the Master's degree level overnight. But the good news is, she moved the way all of us can move. And that is step by step by step by step by step. Little things do make a huge difference.

> I SPEAK WITH CONSIDERABLE CONFIDENCE NOT BECAUSE OF WHAT COMES FROM ME BUT BECAUSE OF WHAT COMES THROUGH ME.

Now I want you to know going in that I validate my statements psychologically, theologically, and physiologically before I verbalize them, write them, or record them because we are physical, we are mental, and we are spiritual. And if we deal with all of those aspects of life, then we are more likely to be on the right path. We are more likely to be right. I speak with considerable confidence not because of what comes *from* me but because of what comes *through* me. There is a huge difference in those two things.

Let me also point out that often and generally I do validate my comments from at least two different sources. When I quoted the statement that my friend had never known a senile person regardless of age, I called my friend Frank at a world-famous clinic filled with psychiatrists and psychologists and asked him if I was right to make the following statement and if he would validate it. I said, "Alzheimer's is a disease, but most mental illnesses are the result of a long series of poor choices." (I said *most* because sometimes illnesses are inherited.) Frank referred me to a doctor who deals with that illness and the doctor said, "Zig, as long as you put it that way, you're absolutely right."

At this particular moment, I don't know where you are in your life, in your career, and your personal, your family, and your business life—and I don't know your past. But Scottish theologian Carl Baade said that *no one can go back and make a new beginning, but all of us can start now and make a new ending.* That's what we're going to be working toward throughout this book.

In many ways, I started when I was forty-five years of age. And the purpose of this book is to give you assurance that yes you can make a new start and new things can happen in an amazing way. My friend Joe says, "You don't have to be great to start, but you have to start to be great." And from my perspective, truer words were never spoken. But people often wonder, *Do I have what it takes to get to the top?*

Years ago I read something that still intrigues me. I read that every third person is either remarkably handsome and amazingly bright—or incredibly beautiful and absolutely brilliant. That person is you! And from this moment on for the rest of your life, if a negative thought ever enters your mind, I want you to say, "No, that's not right about me. I'm an absolutely handsome and smart dude. Or I'm an absolutely beautiful and brilliant gal."

Now consider this—*if you're somebody to anybody, you're somebody.* Think about that just for a moment. Then consider what Mohammed Ali said: "If man can take molded bread and make penicillin out of it, consider what a loving God can make out of you." You were designed for accomplishment and engineered for success. You were endowed with the seeds of greatness. All you have to do is recognize those seeds, water those seeds, and fertilize those seeds. Then you have to realize that you are that third person.

And think about this. Way back in AD 399, Saint Augustine said (I'm paraphrasing) that man travels hundreds of miles to gaze at the broad expanse of the ocean and looks in awe at the heavens above. He stares in wonderment at the fields and the mountains and the rivers and the streams, and then he passes himself by without another thought of God's most amazing creation.

Earthquakes and hurricanes get all the publicity, but did you know that termites do more damage than both of them put together? They take such itty-bitty bites that you can't even see them with the naked eye, but they take so many bites and cause so much damage. The message is this—you can make radical changes in tiny steps. And when you clearly understand that, you start to realize that you can make it to the top, one small step at a time.

> AND THE MOST IMPORTANT OPINION YOU HAVE IS THE OPINION YOU HAVE OF YOURSELF.

I wrote a book of 384 pages. I wrote that book in ten months by writing one and one fourth pages a day, on average, every day for ten months. Radical changes. Small steps. And when we understand that, then some amazing things will happen. How do you go about doing that? Well, a psychologist I frequently quote says, "You can't change from a negative mindset to a positive mindset without changing from negative talking to positive talking." To do that, you must change the input from negative to positive. And *the most important opinion you have is the opinion you have of yourself.* The most important conversation you will have on any day is a conversation you have with yourself—so you need to make your daily conversation very positive.

HOPE AND ACTION

For many years I've talked about my weight loss. For twenty-four years of my adult life, by choice, I weighed well over 200 pounds. I say by choice simply because I've never "accidentally" eaten anything. During those twenty-four years, when I chose to eat too much, I chose to weigh too much. I tried every diet known to man, tried the thirty-day diet—lost a month! But I was determined. I dieted religiously—that means I quit eating in church.

Then in 1972-1973, in a ten-month period of time, I decided to start using my head. I figured out that if I lost one and nine-tenths ounces a day, on average, every day for ten months, I'd lose the thirty-seven pounds I needed to lose. If you have a weight problem, you probably just thought to yourself, *I could do that!* And hope is born! Action always follows hope. No hope—no action. There is hope in the future, there's power in the present, according to my friend John Maxwell.

Years ago, psychotherapist Alfred Adler said, "Hope is the foundational quality of all change because if there is no hope there's no action and the salesperson with no hope of making the sale won't make the call." Why bother? A youngster with no hope won't bother to study: "Why bother, I won't pass anyhow." But give him hope, and action will follow.

That's what this is all about—hope. *Hope is the foundational quality of all change.* Now what we want to do is understand that the doors of opportunity and progress swing open on the hinges of hope. Nations have been discovered because of hope and freed because of hope. There are medical and scientific breakthroughs because of hope. Industries and education acquired because of hope. Cosmetic companies sell hope. Diet programs sell hope. Exercise programs sell hope. Those things are incredibly important.

So everybody wants more of the things that money will buy— well, just about everybody. People who say they're not interested in money lie about other things too. I mean that just happens to be one of the facts of life. Money is not the most important thing in life, but it's reasonably close to oxygen. When you need it, you really do need it. And I'll have to confess that I like the things that money buys. I like to wear nice clothes, drive a nice car, live in a nice house, take that beautiful red-headed wife of mine out to nice restaurants, take nice trips. I like to play golf at the country club. I *like* all of those things and every one of them costs money. But I *love* the things money won't buy.

> ## MONEY CAN BUY ME A BED, BUT IT WON'T BUY ME A GOOD NIGHT'S SLEEP.

Money may buy me a companion, but it won't buy me a friend. Money can buy me a bed, but it won't buy me a good night's sleep. It will buy me a good time, but it won't buy me peace of mind. Those are the things that I really love. We're going to look at how we get *more* of the things that money *will* buy and *all* of the things that money *won't* buy.

WHAT PEOPLE WANT AND NEED

As we go along, we're going to identify the things that people want and need. Everybody wants to be happy and healthy and reasonably prosperous and secure. They want to have friends and peace of mind and good family relationships—and have the hope that their future is going to be even better. But more than that we need love and we need to be loved. Can we take steps to make those things happen? Well, we start with this philosophy—*you can have everything in life you want if you will help enough other people get what they want.*

Contrary to what some people believe, actually you can spend your life any way you want—but you can spend it only once. Just one time—one life to live. If standard of living is your number one priority, quality of life almost never improves. But if quality of life is your number-one priority, your standard of living almost always improves. This is important to understand. I love what my friend the late William Arthur Ward said: "Each of us will one day be judged by our standard of life, not by our standard of living; by our measure of giving, not by our measure of will; by our simple goodness, not by seeming greatness." I believe that is so true.

It's my complete conviction that this message is an absolute necessity if I am going to fulfill some of the obligations I feel toward the people who've been listening to me and reading my books. My book *See You at the Top* was an introduction to what it is to be successful in life and enjoy many of the things that money will buy—and all the things that money won't buy. *So,* you might wonder, *what else is there?*

Well, one of the prime things we considered is what kind of a contribution can you make to others. For years I've stated that *you* can have everything in life you want if you help other people get what *they* want. But what a lot of people don't understand is the way that works regardless of whatever your field might be.

I never will forget when a writer from a medical magazine interviewed me and asked, "How does your statement work in the medical profession?" I kind of laughed and said, "It works perfectly. If I get seriously ill and go to the doctor and he gives me the wrong medicine and I end up dying, I'm not going to be telling anybody about what a great doctor he is. But if he gives me the right treatment and I get up running, I'll guarantee you I'll be telling everybody I know what a good doctor he is. He helped me get what I wanted, and in the process he's going to get more of what he wants because other patients will pick up that message and go forward."

> **YOU CAN HAVE EVERYTHING IN LIFE YOU WANT IF YOU HELP OTHER PEOPLE GET WHAT THEY WANT.**

Another example in a different profession comes to mind. Li Ka-shing, according to *Fortune* magazine several years ago, was one of the ten wealthiest people in the world. He earned his fortune by financing small businesses that had good products, good management, and good leadership—but they were undercapitalized. He found out that the going rate for financing a business was 10 percent ownership of that business. And although he could get 11 or 12 percent of the businesses he financed, his advice to his sons, who now run the business, was that 9 percent of a thriving business was worth much more than 12 percent of a struggling business.

He realized that of far more significance is the fact that when the businesses see he is genuinely interested in them being successful, he will get everything he wants—and they will too. Then the larger business world would see and say, "Hey, you know that Li Ka-shing is really a neat guy. He wants me to be successful!" And as a result, they would send him lots more business.

It's a philosophy that works in your personal life, your family life, your business life—it works absolutely everywhere. That's one of the main things I want to make clear—there is more to life than just having money, more than just being healthy. When you enter into this philosophy, you actually are entering into a spiritual dimension, and that's where real joy comes from. That's where real success comes.

CONTINUE TO GROW

Then there's another factor involved in success too—the fact that we must all continue to grow. You are never static in life; you never stay in one spot. You're either going down or you're going up. If you're not going up then the obvious fact is you are going down in different areas of your life. People need to keep on growing. They need to keep learning. And as discussed later on in the book, your creativity is dependent on always acquiring new information because that makes the old knowledge and information even more usable.

> CREATIVITY IS DEPENDENT ON ALWAYS ACQUIRING NEW INFORMATION BECAUSE THAT MAKES THE OLD KNOWLEDGE AND INFORMATION EVEN MORE USABLE.

The bottom line at the end of all of this is that you will add considerable joy to other people's lives. There's nothing quite like joy, which goes well beyond happiness because happiness often depends on happenings, whereas you can have joy despite the fact that there might be grief in your life. A view from the top can actually come in a dungeon or in a whale because I'm actually talking about your spirit and your attitude—not a physical location. Historically speaking, we know that all great leaders come from adversity, all completely successful people come out of adversity when they go down into the valley and emerge with wisdom.

But as my friend and mentor says, it is when you're in the valley that you grow the food that you're going to eat on the mountaintop. Think about this for a moment: *you can't climb a smooth mountain.* There's so much truth in that statement. You have to have footholds along the way, you have to have those jagged parts that factor in what you're doing; and when you have those, then you have a better view and the view from the top takes you to the mountaintop.

I've been to the mountaintop not only figuratively speaking but literally speaking. I've flown in the Concorde at over 60,000 feet above the earth. And from there you can literally see the curvature of the earth. I was in South Africa, on Cape Point, with my son and the view from there was absolutely magnificent. We looked to the left and we saw the green of the Indian Ocean. We looked to the right and we saw the blue of the Atlantic Ocean. We looked straight ahead and we saw where those two oceans came together and it gave us one of the most beautiful views of what God had done in this universe that you can possibly imagine. Then off to the left again we could see the mountains. We could see so many beautiful things.

You can catch the view from the top, however, wherever you might be if your attitude is right, your purpose in life is right, and you're genuinely interested in doing things that will make a significant difference in other lives.

LOOK INTO THE END ZONE

The view from the top is a unique position to be in. And if you think about it, its significance is involved when you become a team player as well. One of my favorite stories has to do with the year that Green Bay and Denver were in the Super Bowl. Denver won the game, but the interesting thing is at the beginning of the NFL football season, there were 1,580 players on the opening day rosters. Forty-four of those players came from Notre Dame, thirty-six of those players came from Penn State. Now please understand there are hundreds of schools that play football. And yet if you put your pencil to it, over 5 percent of them came from only two schools. Now why and how did that happen?

Well interestingly enough, those are the only two major schools who do not put the names of the players on their jerseys. Why is that important? It's very simple if you think about it. In all of football, the quarterback, the wide receiver, the running back—those are the guys who get all of the attention and all of the recognition. But any coach worth his salt will tell you that the offensive tackle is key to winning the game, as is the defensive end, as is the quarterback, as is the center. In other words, the eleven players on offense and the eleven players on defense constitute a winning football team if they are playing together as a team.

NOW INDIVIDUALS DO SCORE POINTS, BUT TEAMS WIN GAMES.

So when the names are not on the jerseys, that simply means that the attention is drawn to the player with the number on his back and that player get the recognition he deserves. As a matter of fact, the Penn State football team has always had a very simple rule. When the *team* scores a touchdown, the individual who has the ball in his hand when he crosses the goal line is to hand the ball back to the official, go back to the huddle and say, "Thanks guys, you all did your job." The *team* is the winner.

Now individuals do score points, but teams win games. When you're a producing member of a team, recognizing the value and importance of all the others will add a significant portion to your own life and to the team and enables you not only to live well but finish well. I assure you from that point of view, you will enjoy your view from the top very much because you've been part of a winning team.

The view from the top comes to people who've done significant things. Now that does not necessarily mean it comes from a corporate position. For example, I don't know if Mother Teresa would have made it on Wall Street, but I do know she made it big time in life. A lot of people confuse success with fame. Madonna had fame. Mother Teresa had success. A view from the top enables people to experience real success that makes a difference not only in their own lives but in the lives of many other people.

WHAT MONEY BUYS

People who spend a lot of time watching television or reading the newspapers or the society pages get the idea that successful people get a lot of recognition. They read that some billionaire donated a million dollars to some charitable cause and that's a wonderful thing to do. But they look at those individuals as being successful as a result of their financial accomplishments. I will share with you some information that I believe will open your eyes.

In 1923, there was a meeting at the Edgewater Beach Hotel in Chicago of some of the most powerful and influential people in the world at that time. The group included, for example, the president of the largest independent steel company, the president of the largest utility company, the president of the largest gas company, the president of the New York Stock Exchange, a member of the president's cabinet, the greatest "bear" on Wall Street, the head of the world's greatest monopoly, also the president of the Bank of International Settlements. Certainly, these men were tremendously accomplished. They had a lot of recognition and a tremendous amount of money and power.

But let's look at what happened to those men later in life. One of those men went insane. Two ended up penniless at the end of their lives. Three committed suicide, and two spent some time in prison. Now I ask you, were these men successful in life or just financially successful? From my perspective, I wouldn't swap places with any one of them. And I'll bet you wouldn't either.

Significance with a view from the top looks at life from a different perspective. Later in this book we will discuss people who earned a lot of money and had a lot of influence, but they also had balance in their lives. Those are the successful people. Those are the ones with a view from the top.

CHARACTER MATTERS

Almost from the very beginning of my life I was considered somewhat of a rebel. And by that I simply mean I did not play the game as everybody necessarily thought the game should be played. As a youngster I got into a lot of fights because I could not stand to see a bully take advantage of a smaller child. And on many occasions, though it appeared to be none of my business, I got involved and I defended the smaller child or the one who was less athletically inclined. That was a sign of rebellion. Now I have to confess, in all fairness, I enjoyed fighting.

Along the way I've talked a great deal about character. In the past ten years there have been a lot of people who maintained that character really didn't count. As long as you could do the job, that was the only thing that really mattered to anybody. Well the reality is, when you have a character issue, character does count in the way you do your job at home, on the job, and in society. A good character reflects your life values, which will make you a good husband and father or a good mother and wife. These are the same values that will stand you in wonderful stead in corporate America, on the job whether you are in business for yourself or whether you are part of a large organization.

The reality is, virtually all great failures are character failures. All you have to do is read today's newspaper or tomorrow's newspaper, and you'll see exactly what I'm talking about. *Trust, character, balance in life—if you have them, they will enable you to have a view from the top.* And I'm telling you, you're going to like the view.

CHAPTER 2

IT'S ALL ABOUT BALANCE

You're at the top when you're secure in who you are and are at peace with God and in fellowship with others.

How do you get it all? There's a formula. You start with the right attitude, you have specific skills, and you follow the Golden Rule philosophy, and then you put all of that on a character base and what you have is an honest, legitimate shot at complete success.

Would you deliberately hire an accountant or a treasurer who admitted that he or she was just "relatively honest"? I profess that some things are right, some things are wrong. My wife and I will soon celebrate our fifty-fifth wedding anniversary. And you know in all of those years, not one time have I ever come home and she looked me and asked, "Now honey, tell me the truth. Were you relatively faithful to me while you were gone?" I repeat—some things are right and some things are wrong.

ATTITUDE MATTERS

Character really does count—and your attitude obviously counts too. What is attitude? For example, how do you *respond* or *react* to life when something bad happens? Do you stomp your foot and scream and shout and holler, or do you respond? *Responding is positive.* For example, you get sick and go to the doctor and she gives you a prescription and says, "Take this and I'll see you tomorrow." You walk in the next day and she looks at you and smiles and says, "Hey it's working! Your body is *responding* to treatment." But if you say you're not any better, in fact, you're feeling worse, then the doctor knows that your body is *reacting* to the prescription. Responding makes all the difference within those who do great things and those who do things that are not so great.

Now let me tell you about 300 world-class leaders. I'm talking about people like Mahatma Gandhi, Martin Luther King Jr., Franklin Roosevelt—people like Winston Churchill, Clara Barton, Helen Keller, and Mother Teresa. Of those 300 world-class leaders, 75 percent of them were either raised in poverty, abused as children, or had some physical defect. As serious as their early lives were, they understood that it is not what happens *to* you; what makes the difference is how you *handle* what happens to you. The attitude of responding rather than reacting makes a world of difference in your life. *The good news is simply this: you can control your attitude.*

> ## THE GOOD NEWS IS SIMPLY THIS: YOU CAN CONTROL YOUR ATTITUDE.

When I was in the seventh grade, I tried out for the boxing team. Since I had been a "playground gladiator," I figured I was going to do well. I was matched with Joe, a little kid about sixty-two pounds, and I was eighty-two pounds so I felt kind of sorry for the little guy. Well, that sympathy for him lasted all of about four or five, maybe six seconds into the first round. I had forgotten that Joe had been with the boxing team for two years and I'd been on a playground in slugfests. I found out quickly that there is a big difference.

Joe was pretty good at math because he figured out the shortest distance from his glove to the end of my nose was a short, left jab. He thought I was a slow learner because he did it again and again and again and again. The coach put a stop to the slaughter, took me aside, and started teaching me some of the fundamentals of boxing.

At the end of two weeks, because of the twenty-pound weight advantage and the skills I learned, I was able to hold my own. I learned through that experience that *positive thinking won't let you do anything, but it will let you do everything better than negative thinking will.* And when you add skill to positive thinking, then you've taken a huge step forward.

Attitude can change the way you look at things. Have you ever had one of *those* days? I mean when everything that could go wrong did go wrong? Mercifully the day ends and you head home. You walk in the door and your wife greets you with considerable enthusiasm, "Can't wait to get started on cleaning the garage!" she says. You say, "Oh no, that's not today, is it? I just can't muster any energy, dear." She pleads, "It'll only take about three or four hours. We can get it finished in no time. I'll meet you out there."

About that time the telephone rings, and with your last ounce of energy you stumble over and pick it up with both hands. The voice at the other end says, "Hey, pal! I just got us a tee time at the club in fifteen minutes. Can you make it?" You respond, "Can I make it? I'll be there in ten minutes!" Let me ask you a ridiculous question: what if you had the same attitude toward cleaning the garage as going golfing? If you had the same positive attitude toward doing tasks you don't like to do as the ones you like, how would that change your life? What would that do for your career? Your marriage? What would that do to every facet of your life? When we can develop a positive attitude, we absolutely can accomplish much.

THE RIGHT WORDS

Charles Osgood, the CBS word merchant, said compared to the spoken word a picture is a pitiful thing. Indeed, words will pick you up or put you down. A little girl said it better than anybody I've ever heard when she said, "Sticks and stones may break my bones, but words can break my heart." The words Churchill used are the reason that we have the freedom we have today—words spoken demanded freedom. I want to emphasize that we need to use the right words, always.

When you have the character base and the right attitude in life, for permanent performance, it's important to know that character gets you out of bed, commitment moves you to action, faith, hope, discretion, and discipline enable you to follow through to completion.

How do you build character? It can be taught; you can learn it. I've been privileged to serve on the National Board of the Boy Scouts of America for five years. I well remember on Thursday nights how many times I stood up and said, "On my *honor*—beautiful word—I will do my best to do my duty to God and my country, and obey the Scout law, to help other people at all times, to keep myself physically strong, mentally awake, and morally straight." That's self-talk, talking about character. The Boy Scout law is for a Scout to be trustworthy, loyal, helpful, friendly, courteous, kind, obedient, cheerful, thrifty, brave, clean, and reverent. The Scout motto is: Be prepared! The Boy Scout slogan is: Do a good turn [deed] daily! Now what are the benefits of all those words that build character? Let's look at some of the benefits kids see after being involved in scouting.

Ninety-eight percent of them, according to the Harris poll in 1995, finished high school. Forty percent finished college versus 16 percent of the general population. Thirty-three percent earned $50,000 a year or more versus just 17 percent of those who were not involved in scouting. I spoke to a judge several years ago and he said, "Zig, I have never had a juvenile in front of me being charged with some kind of crime or misdemeanor who has been in scouting a year or more. Not even one."

Is character a quality that makes a difference in life? I believe with all my heart that yes indeed these traits do count and they count big time. Ninety-four percent of these kids said that what they learned in scouting affected their values all the rest of their lives.

> THERE'S NO GUILT WITH INTEGRITY AND THERE'S NOTHING TO FEAR, BECAUSE YOU HAVE NOTHING TO HIDE.

What is it that everybody wants? To be happier, healthier, reasonably prosperous, and secure. They want to have friends, peace of mind, good family relationships, hope that the future's going to be better, and they need to love and be loved. Now to get all of these things, you have to deal with *all* of yourself. You have to be the right kind of person. You have to do the right thing in order to have all that life has to offer.

With a character-based life and integrity, you do the right thing. There's no guilt with integrity and there's nothing to fear, because you have nothing to hide. When you take fear and guilt off your back, you are free to be your best self and do your best work on the job and with your family. If you're going to have all that life has to offer now, you also have to look at not only the financial aspects but also the physical, mental, and spiritual.

It's true that people *without* character and integrity can possess cars and houses and vacations, but good people *with* character and integrity can have so much more. They can have all the things money can buy *plus* all the things that money can't buy.

Evaluate Yourself

Now you need to evaluate where you are right now. It's important for you to know where you are because that's the most effective and most certain way of determining where you want to go and how you're going to get there. As I go through this little process, I want you to grade yourself.

Several years ago, Steve was in my office. He was there because a friend of his had flown him from Toronto, Canada, because Steve had the wrong role models, the wrong hero. He was following a guy considered to be the most successful man he had ever known.

Steve left home every morning at 6 o'clock and returned home every night between 10 and 11—six days a week. On Sunday he was so exhausted that he slept all day had no family life. He had run off the road two or three times driving back and forth twenty or thirty miles every day one way. Everything was falling apart; his wife was threatening to divorce him.

> **IT'S IMPORTANT FOR YOU TO KNOW WHERE YOU ARE BECAUSE THAT'S THE MOST EFFECTIVE AND MOST CERTAIN WAY OF DETERMINING WHERE YOU WANT TO GO AND HOW YOU'RE GOING TO GET THERE.**

I had been forewarned of all of this and so I said to Steve, "I understand you have a hero, and that your boss is your hero because he's successful. How do you define success?"

It took him a few minutes but he finally said, "Well, I think success is when you're happy and healthy—and have friends and peace of mind and good family relationships and the hope that the future is going to be even better."

I said, "Okay. Well now let's do something most people don't do—evaluate yourself." A lot of people won't do that because they're afraid they might find something they don't like. But we need to face facts. Reader, as I relay this conversation to you that I had with Steve, I challenge you to evaluate yourself as we go along.

I said to Steve, "Let's look at your boss according to the things you said make a person successful—happiness, good health, friends, peace of mind, good family relationships, and the hope for a better future."

I asked Steve, "Do you think your boss is happy?"

"No, not really. I never heard him laugh and he seldom smiles. And he has ulcers."

"Well, Steve, seems to me your boss isn't happy, or healthy, and if he has ulcers, he must not have peace of mind."

They say that insanity is the belief that you can keep on doing what you've been doing—but somehow think you can get different results. It's not going to happen!

I asked, "Steve, how prosperous is your boss?"

He said, "Man, he's got money running out of his ears."

"Is he secure?"

"He's as secure as money can make him."

Steve was equating security in life with how much money a person has in the bank and a corporate position. I told him about the billionaire brothers in Dallas who went bankrupt, an industrialist worth half a billion and a former governor worth a hundred million—and they all went bankrupt.

Then I asked Steve how many friends his boss had. He said, "Really, I don't think he has any. And I'm not his friend. I just admire him because he's so successful. But to tell you the truth, the guy is somewhat of a jerk."

Then I asked, "Tell me about his family."

"Well, his wife's divorcing him."

"And how much hope for the future does your boss have?"

"Well, before I started talking to you I thought he had a lot of hope, but now I don't think he has any *real* hope."

"Steve, let me ask you a question. Would you swap places with your boss right now?"

"No."

Now I ask you, reader, the same question. Would you swap places with Steve's boss?

The answer would emphatically be no, would it not?

Three or four years later, I was speaking in Baltimore, Maryland, and a young man came to me and asked, "Do you remember me?" And even though I have a brilliant memory, it's awful short. So I said, "I'm sorry, but really I don't."

He said, "I'm Steve from Toronto and I took your advice—that I didn't have to work seventy to eighty hours a week to be successful. As a matter of fact, when I brought my life into *balance*, I was more productive, more creative, and could do more things. I took your advice and got a better job with far fewer hours and much better pay. I was able to go back and love my wife and family again and I wanted to show you some *real* growth." I don't carry many pictures in my wallet but I have one of Steve and his family...and the little addition to the family who arrived after we had our meeting.

> ## WHEN I BROUGHT MY LIFE INTO BALANCE, I WAS MORE PRODUCTIVE, MORE CREATIVE, AND COULD DO MORE THINGS.

I'm not in the speaking, training, or book business. I'm in the life-changing business. Why was Steve able to do so much more? Something happens when you understand one of the very basic elements of life—*life values,* the qualities that make you a great husband and father or a great wife and mother. Qualities that make you great at home are also the qualities that are so critical on the job. When you develop all of those qualities, they bring balance to your life. That's what Steve did.

EVERYTHING STARTS WITH YOU

The reality is, everything starts with you. It's your personal responsibility. Your personal life affects your family life, which affects your business life, which affects you physically, which affects you mentally, which affects you spiritually, which affects you financially, which affects you personally.

You can take any two of those and they will affect each other. Your family life affects your spiritual life. Your physical life affects the financial. The personal affects the mental. Everything affects everything else; and when you bring it all together, synergy develops.

Why am I excited about all this? Because when I left home today, the last thing I did was get a big hug from my wife. And she hugged me back, twice actually, and said, "I love you." I don't have to worry about what's going on there when I'm gone. I don't have to worry about the telephone ringing at night. I don't have to worry about someone coming in and saying, "I'm from the government." We don't have to worry about those things. Why? Because when you play it straight, synergy takes place in all of your life. Having it all? Yes, you can have it all.

All includes employment security in a no-job-security world. Not only can we have employment security in a no-job-security world, we can go *up* in the down-sizing world. I hope you're enjoying your view from the top so far.

> I'M NOT IN THE SPEAKING, TRAINING, OR BOOK BUSINESS. I'M IN THE LIFE-CHANGING BUSINESS.

CHAPTER 3

MOVING FROM SUCCESS
TO SIGNIFICANCE

Many people in our society today believe that we need to separate the various phases of our lives, such as our personal life from our business life. They believe we should have "compartments." Let's talk about that because it is very, very important. Number one, I don't believe you can or should compartmentalize your life if you're going to enjoy total success.

I believe strongly in *focus*. This is one of the reasons *integrity* and *character* play such an important part in what you do. With integrity you do the right thing. And when you do the right thing, you don't have any guilt. With integrity, you have nothing to fear because you have nothing to hide. Now think about this for a moment, when you take fear and guilt off your shoulders, you can do so many more things.

When we look at our family life, if we live with integrity there, and then take that same integrity into the business world, when we're at home we can concentrate on what we do at home. And when we're on the job, we can concentrate on what we do on the job. We've made certain that our foundation is absolutely solid. We don't have to worry about what's going on somewhere else. As a result, because we have *not* compartmentalized our life, we are able to focus on whatever it is we are doing and be more successful. We have greater peace of mind, more friends, better family relationships, and more stable associations with the people we work with. We become teammates, supporters and encouragers of each other, and actually all of this enhances our performance on the job. This all leads to a balanced life.

Success as Significance

I define success as significance. How do you achieve one and then translate it into the other? First of all, *success is maximizing the gifts and potential you have.* When you maximize your gifts and potential, you can accomplish worthwhile objectives and enjoy some of the things that money will buy—and *all* of the things that money won't buy.

Success comes in a lot of different colors and a lot of different ways in a lot of different lives. The individual with a minimum amount of ability who is able to earn an honest living, I believe that is a successful person. It's been discovered that people with low incomes donate a higher percentage of their income to charity. They recognize that others have even less than they do.

> **SUCCESS IS MAXIMIZING THE GIFTS AND POTENTIAL YOU HAVE.**

I believe these people move into *significance* when they take that step, and joy comes from helping other people. It's the Golden Rule in operation. Significance encompasses a spiritual dimension, and a spiritual dimension always involves care and concern for another person. When you look at the way society is today, with all of the conflict we have, you know we've become an "Hooray for me and to heck with you. I'm going to do it my way" world. I've just described a person who is self-centered, selfish, not caring about other people—and you will never find one of these people who are truly happy.

Parents need to teach children life values and honorable qualities early on in life to build their character base. Doing a good deed every day usually means doing something nice for somebody else.

Karl Menninger, of the Menninger Clinic, said if you have a problem, you need to go find someone with a bigger problem, get involved in helping that person solve the problem, and lo and behold, *your* problem will disappear. It's going to be solved. A *Psychology Today* article stated that people who are active in their communities—volunteer to feed the homeless and do things that help other people—are, interestingly enough, more successful in their own business and lives because they are energized—physiologically energized—when they do something for other people. In the process of doing something for others, they feel so good about themselves that their energy level goes up; and as a result, they can do a great deal more in their own personal and business lives, as well as with their families.

> SIGNIFICANCE ENCOMPASSES A SPIRITUAL DIMENSION, AND A SPIRITUAL DIMENSION ALWAYS INVOLVES CARE AND CONCERN FOR ANOTHER PERSON.

One of the interesting things about Alcoholics Anonymous is that you'll often find a day laborer counseling the president of a company. The day laborer has whipped the alcohol problem—the president of the company has not. Alcoholics have told me that when they're called, they must go and help the person who has screamed for help. Invariably, something spiritual happens to the individual who stays up all night long helping. Although the helper should be absolutely exhausted the next day, in most cases, the person is completely energized and even more productive—even after staying up all night. Something happens to people when they do something really significant in somebody else's life.

THE DAY BEFORE VACATION

As a general rule, people get about twice as much work done on the day before they go on vacation. Why? Well, if we can figure out why and learn how and repeat that process every day without working any longer or any harder—does it make sense that we will be more valuable to ourselves, our jobs, our families, and our communities.

On the day before a vacation, most get out their laptop or a sheet of paper write down what needs to be done—they set goals. If that's you, then you organize the list in the order of importance. You then accept responsibility and make a commitment to do everything on the list. I've noticed, though, that a lot of people are about as committed as a kamikaze pilot on his thirty-ninth mission!

But you are different, you care about the people who aren't going on vacation; you're a dependable employee. It shows you work with integrity. You want to do what's right. You work smarter not harder. You're optimistic that you're going to get the job done. Have you ever participated in organized team sports?

When you know the coach had a good game plan, something happened to your thinking. You knew what you had to do and you were optimistic.

On the day before vacation, you were punctual and you immediately got busy. You didn't stand around and wonder what to do next. You were enthusiastic about what you were doing and you were highly motivated. You decisively moved from one step to another, one task to the next.

Have you ever noticed that as a general rule, when you are moving with purpose through your game plan that people step aside and let you go by? They're not going to stand in your way to gossip and listen to stories about what's going on behind the scenes in the office. And incidentally, from my perspective, the most guilty of the two is not the one spreading the gossip, it's the one who who's listening, because if there's no one receiving it, there's no conversation.

If you haven't noticed already from previous "day before vacations," you'll be amazed at how much time you save and how much you accomplish. Three minutes here, four minutes there, and at the end of the day I will absolutely guarantee you that just because you move with purpose, you will have saved an hour that day. And if you work like that every day, at an hour a day, that's five hours a week, which is 250 hours a year, which is more than six weeks you have carved out! And a lot more than that really, because you haven't wasted the time of the one you want to gossip with you.

Decisiveness and Positive Thinking

Decisiveness also is a sign of leadership. You get the information and you make the decision and you go full speed ahead. You focus on what's at hand and you discipline yourself to take the necessary action until you get it done. Discipline is most sorely missing in most people's lives. You build momentum and a positive attitude kicks in. I get a little upset with individuals who say, "With positive thinking you can do just about anything!" Although I'm a very positive person, that statement is absolutely not true. And the following supports that statement.

> **DECISIVENESS ALSO IS A SIGN OF LEADERSHIP.**

I love to play golf. I'm pretty good at it. I shot my age about four months ago and I'm seventy-four; and even better news is it didn't take me but thirteen holes to do it. I know I can play better but I never have. I have fun playing golf, but there is absolutely no danger that I'm going to qualify for the PGA. Now I have a *great* attitude, but I don't have the skills to follow through. And I had a good attitude when I went in the ring with Joe back when I was a kid. I knew I was going to whip that sixty-two-pounder. But I didn't have the skills to follow through. I learned the skill of

47

boxing; I acquired the skill. I've been trying for years to acquire the skill to play golf but it just hasn't happened. My positive attitude, though, makes me honestly believe that my next game is going to be the best game ever.

Positive thinking is critically important. That's what you're using on the day before vacation. *Positive thinking doesn't let you do anything, but it will let to do everything better.* Thinking positively enables you to use that knowledge you've acquired, the experience you've acquired, the training you've had, to use what you already know. That's awesome! Your performance, competency, and confidence increase and you become an "extra-miler"—the person who goes the extra mile. That individual is always desirable in the marketplace. You're a team player.

You're an encourager.

People look at your example and they don't realize it but they instinctively step up their production themselves. They move just a little faster, with a little more purpose, with less delay. Not only will your productivity go dramatically higher, but the whole company will raise their standards 2, 3, 5 percent and every bit of that goes to the bottom line. Management will notice. And talk about employment security? They will want to keep you around.

With a positive attitude and decisiveness driving you, at the end of the day your energy level is absolutely off the wall. On the way home you're talking to yourself, "Man, I had more fun than I ever had. I can't wait to get home and tell the family. Matter of fact, I think we're going to pack up tonight and go on vacation. Why wait till tomorrow!" You know exactly what I'm talking about, don't you?

> ## WITH A POSITIVE ATTITUDE AND DECISIVENESS DRIVING YOU, AT THE END OF THE DAY YOUR ENERGY LEVEL IS ABSOLUTELY OFF THE WALL.

When are you most exhausted at the end of the day? When you tried to fool the boss all day. Or if you are the boss, you tried to fool the troops all day. Or how about doing nothing all day—that's one of the most exhausting days you'll ever have. But when you're on a mission and determined to complete your list and you're making progress every hour that passes, not only does your self-worth increase, you also feel good about yourself. Hope is raised to its full bloom because you're being *wise* all the way through each task.

KNOWLEDGE AND WISDOM

Of course, you can get information and gain knowledge from newspapers, magazines, good books, and encyclopedias—but wisdom is a gift from God. And you use wisdom in this process of journeying to the top because you're being the right kind of person, you're doing the right thing that enables you to have all of the things that life has to offer. I emphasize this point: you cannot expect to live like this one day a year and receive success and significance.

Notice that I haven't mentioned a word about working harder. I'm talking about fulfilling the responsibility you accepted when you got the job. I'm talking about working smarter. I'm talking about being a role model. I'm talking about your future. It's exciting that when you evaluate what you've done, you see passion is born when you catch a glimpse of your possibilities. That's what you do on this day before vacation.

So, let me ask you a question: if organizing and planning one day made such a huge impact on your performance, does it make sense that if you planned every day, good things would continue to happen?

YOU SEE PASSION IS BORN WHEN YOU CATCH A GLIMPSE OF YOUR POSSIBILITIES. THAT'S WHAT YOU DO ON THIS DAY BEFORE VACATION.

Employment Security

In case you are at this moment looking for a job, let me tell you some interesting facts. As I write this, there are 132 million Americans who are gainfully employed. We also know that every year there is a 21 percent turnover in jobs, simply meaning that 21 percent of those people are working on a job this moment that they did not have last year. As a matter of fact, some of them weren't working at all.

Now let's look at it on a very realistic basis. That simply means 21 percent of the 132 million is well over 27 million people who are now in a job they did not have a year ago. Now what that boils down to is the fact that every month more than 1 million people find new jobs. That means over 500,000 find new jobs every week. That means over 100,000 people find a job every single day. If you're unemployed, you'd like to get one of those 100,000 jobs that are going to be filled today. When you go out, go out with a complete assurance and confidence and optimism and enthusiasm and all the motivation you can muster. Go out with a conviction that you have the skills, talent, commitment, responsibility, and the qualities that will make you a valued employee.

You might not get your dream job the first time you fill out an application. But I've discovered that is it is easier to get a good job if you're currently employed. Don't be so particular or persnickety that you won't take a job because it's beneath your dignity. You don't have to go to the bottom of the totem pole. You can, though, accept a job that might not be exactly what you want, seeing it as a springboard to get what you want. And here's another interesting fact—the job that you look down on at the moment might turn into your dream job.

And another little bit of statistical data you might be impressed with is that from 1989 to 1995—yes, I know the economy was booming during those years—but did you know that 15 million new businesses were created in that period of time? Did you know that way over half of them were created by women? Many of them did not have the skill, experience, or background that would qualify them to start their own business. In many cases, it was a desperation move as they had been divorced or widowed and left with children, so they had to do something—so they started their own business.

Now here's what fascinates me about this. Most of those jobs created as a result of starting those new businesses were *trust* jobs. The women offered goods and or services, but they said, you pay me now and I'll deliver later. And according to the article I read in the *Wall Street Journal,* there was no record of any of those women being prosecuted for failure to deliver the promises they had made. In other words, they were trustworthy. They delivered. And that is one of the reasons they're successful today.

When you go looking, if you can't find what you want and you have a few bucks laid aside, you might want to consider your own business. There are a lot of sources such as the Small Business Administration that can be helpful. Mentors can help you. The employer where you worked before, etc. So go out every day with optimism, excitement, and enthusiasm—get that job or start that new business because that's the way you will ultimately love your view from the top.

> **GO OUT EVERY DAY WITH OPTIMISM, EXCITEMENT, AND ENTHUSIASM— GET THAT JOB OR START THAT NEW BUSINESS BECAUSE THAT'S THE WAY YOU WILL ULTIMATELY LOVE YOUR VIEW FROM THE TOP.**

SELF-TALK

Before you go to bed tonight, get in front of a mirror and start talking to yourself. Say something like, "I'm YOUR NAME. I'm an honest person. I'm intelligent. I have my goals (LIST THEM one by one, claiming every one of them) and I will accomplish each one." The more you claim them the more you will believe them and they will come to pass. This concept goes way back to biblical times where self-talk was first started. It's not something brand-new in psychology today. It's been proven that what you say to yourself is extraordinarily important.

*But you got to **be,** before you can **do,** and do, before you can **have**.* And every one of these qualities—character, integrity, confidence, wisdom, positive thinking, going the extra mile, decisiveness—and many, many more are already qualities you have. With these qualities reigning in you, you will have the privilege of looking at life with a view from the top.

CHAPTER 4

BUILDING WINNING RELATIONSHIPS

You're at the top when you clearly understand that failure is an event, not a person.

I love the story of a man who walked into a bookstore and walked up to the manager and said, "Ma'am, can you tell me where I can find the book, *Man, the Superior Sex?*" She said, "Oh yes, it's upstairs in the science fiction department." When we clearly understand that there is no superior sex, that there is no superior race, then we will have laid the foundation for building winning relationships with all people in our job, community, nation, and in this global world we live in today.

Let me bring this truth to a very personal level. The five people who had the most impact on my life were all women. Do you really think those women would have had a huge interest in my life if I had I been sexist? Three Native Americans had a huge impact on my life. One in my sales career, one in my speaking career, and one in my spiritual walk. I'm a Christian today because an elderly African-American lady spent the weekend in our home on July 4, 1972.

My closest friend for the past thirty-seven years is Jewish. Our director of international operations is from India. My daughter-in-law is from Mexico. I'm affiliated with a very large Japanese company with a Korean president. My son-in-law just had a liver transplant. We never asked if the donor was black, white, brown, or anything in between. My doctors tell me that we're all the same color inside.

I shudder to think what my life would have been like had I been racist—it would have been absolutely horrible. And now the DNA shows that Adam and Eve really did start it all. So that person next to you really is kinfolk—and if you're going to spend eternity with them, you might as well get along with them now. Since relationships factor into everything we do, I'm going to share what I've learned about relationships and what impact they have on every aspect of our lives.

A twenty-year Harvard study concluded that your relationships have more to do with your physical health than the food you eat, the exercise program you're on, and even the genes you have inherited. As a general rule, if you are getting along with the people you love most, regardless of the condition of your bank account and your occupation, basically you're reasonably happy. If you're not getting along well with the people you love, it doesn't make any difference how much money you have in the bank or how high you are on the totem pole; basically you're not very happy.

BUILDING
WINNING RELATIONSHIPS

Nearly 100 percent of all of counseling is done because of relationship difficulties. Difficulties between husband and wife, parent and child, teacher and student, employer and employee, etc. There's a lot of relationship difficulties among the races as well. Think of all the problems caused simply because we've not built winning relationships. Now let's take a look at what we can do to build those winning relationships. First of all, we need to have a philosophy.

A psychologist said that 80 percent of all the family counseling he did was because the parents had not taught their children manners. Manners are more than how to hold a knife and fork. It is deportment, civility, respect, and concern for other people. The parent who does not teach, demand, and require that their child say please and especially thank you when somebody says something nice about them or does something nice is denying their child the building block of *gratitude, which is the healthiest of all human emotion.* Those children will grow up expecting the world to pay them the living that they feel is deserved. They will grow up as fair-weather friends, meaning they're only there when *they* need *you*. They expect you to do things for them and they're absolutely miserable as a result of it. They suffer terribly.

You will never see a happy self-centered person. The happy people are the givers. Let's consider a little scenario. It starts on Friday afternoon in this scenario. The husband has been gone all week long. He comes to the front porch about 6 o'clock heavy laden with luggage and briefcase. Doesn't want to set it down to ring the doorbell, so he kicks the door a couple of times. Then he kicks it harder—bang, bang, bang, bang. The wife comes running to the door, opens it, and sees him standing there.

He doesn't move, he just looks at her and says, "The reason I'm late is because I've been to a meeting. Boy, I'm sure glad I went to that meeting because I learned some things that really bug me. I learned that there are some rights around this house that I have not been getting. As a matter of fact, I have made a list of them and the first thing we're gonna do, old woman, is we're gonna sit down and talk. We're going to go over this list because there's gonna be some changes made around here!"

I can well imagine her responding, "Well, Buster, I didn't go to a meeting. I didn't need to. And I have not written a list. I didn't need to do that either. I've got burned indelibly in the mind what needs to change. You come on in and we are going to talk. I agree with you there are going to be some changes made around here—and you're not gonna like most of them!"

Now let your imagination run wild. Don't you know this couple had an absolutely incredible weekend. Don't you know they had an idyllic, loving, romantic weekend. Don't you know that they became so inspired about their wonderful weekend together that they couldn't wait until Monday morning to get out there and change the world—to help make it a better place to live.

Now let's consider the same person, same scenario—but with a different attitude and different words. The husband comes to the front porch laden with the luggage and briefcase that he didn't want to set down, so he gently taps the door with his foot. His wife comes to the door and opens it. The man walks in and says, "Sweetheart, I'm late because I went to a meeting and I'll be forever grateful that I went because I learned some things that really bother me. I learned that in all probability as a husband I have not been meeting your needs as my wife. Before I even unpack, I want us to talk. I want you to tell me what can I do to become the kind of husband you thought you were getting and you deserve to have."

I can well imagine her response, "Well actually, I've been very happy being your wife. From time to time I've wondered if I'm meeting all of *your* needs."

Now I ask you: Which couple do you think will have greater contributions to make as individuals to our society? Which couple will not only experience happiness but joy in their lives? Which couple do you think will raise the happiest, healthiest, most productive, progressive, good citizens?

THE GOLDEN RULE

I'm totally convinced that you can have everything in life you want—if you will help enough other people get what they want. It's our responsibility to put the other person first. The Golden Rule is still in force—do to others as you would have them do to you. So many times people say about our society's ills, "Well, why don't *they* do something!" Well, *they* is *you.* You were born to win—but only if you plan to win and prepare to win can you legitimately expect to win. I'll tell you that winning is simple, but I'll never tell you that winning is easy. Your attitude for the next person you meet will make all the difference in the world to that person.

> ## I'LL TELL YOU THAT WINNING IS SIMPLE, BUT I'LL NEVER TELL YOU THAT WINNING IS EASY.

We've identified nine things everybody wants in life: 1) to be happy, 2) healthy, 3) reasonably prosperous, 4) secure, 5) have friends, 6) peace of mind, 7) good family relationships, 8) hope that the future is going to be better. We also need to be loved and to love others. How can you get people to love you? Be the right kind of person. When you go out looking for friends, they will be hard to find. But if you go out looking to be a friend, you will find them everywhere.

It has been said that we affect 10,000 people directly or indirectly during our lifetime. I've heard it said that no raindrop ever blames itself for the flood. No snowflake ever blames itself for the blizzard—and yet each played a part. I have on the wall in my office the photographs of twenty-six men and women. I call it my wall of gratitude. These men and women had a huge impact on my life. I want you to think it through and have your own wall of gratitude. It will impact your life positively.

Play it back in your own mind who has helped you. Who was there when you needed some help? Which man, woman, teacher, pet, neighbor, employer, member of your church—put up photos as reminders of those who have helped you along the way.

Now there's always a possibility that your life really is not what you want it to be right now or where you want it to be. But maybe it's not your fault.

Consider this hypothetical example. You've been saving your money and finally have enough to build a home of your dreams. You hired an architect with an incredible, worldwide reputation to design the house, and he did. You found the number-one builder of luxury homes in that whole area. He followed the instructions the architect gave and used all of the exact materials, the very best of everything. The home was finished and it was absolutely beautiful. You moved in and had a big celebration party. Everybody came and said what a wonderful place.

About six weeks later, a slight crack appeared in one of the walls. Two months later you looked and saw that the crack was bigger. Then almost on a daily basis there were more cracks. The house started to crumble in less than a year. Eventually, the building code required that the house be abandoned. Now I ask you, whose fault was it? Was it the architect who designed the plan or the builder who followed the plan exactly as prescribed? Who would you blame? The architect? Absolutely. If you're not as far along as you'd like to be in life—maybe you've been listening to the wrong plans from the wrong person.

Years ago on a TV talk show, a Hollywood star was being interviewed. The host asked her, "How do you hold on to a man?" This woman had been married so many times she had rice marks on her face. She was the wrong person to ask such a question. All too often we take advice from people equally poorly qualified. So we need to devise a game plan that enables us to build healthy relationships—on a solid foundation. Regardless of how many wonderful qualities you might have, if you don't have the right game plan, good things are not going to happen in the use of those qualities.

You have to be in the right position, and you start by understanding first of all that *failure is an event, not a person.* Yesterday really did end last night and sometimes an apparent failure maybe is not a failure after all. For example, the Edsel automobile was considered the greatest failure Ford Motor Company ever produced. It was ugly, not very many sold, and there was only one model. I'm here to make the case for a different view. I think it was their greatest success because out of that technology the Mustang was produced, and from that technology the Taurus was produced. The two most popular and profitable motor cars Ford ever built, at the time of this writing. We never want to miss the good in a bad experience; we need to look for the good in each particular situation. Remember, *you can't go back and make a new beginning, but you start now to make a new ending.*

> **IF YOU'RE NOT AS FAR ALONG AS YOU'D LIKE TO BE IN LIFE—MAYBE YOU'VE BEEN LISTENING TO THE WRONG PLANS FROM THE WRONG PERSON.**

PICTURE YOURSELF

Now I want to emphasize a point—we are attracted to the strongest picture that goes into our minds. It is very important to be careful about the pictures we allow into our minds—especially the visuals we see on television and in the movies—because we are affected by what goes into our minds. For example, the pictures we paint as parents are very important. We talk about the "terrible twos" instead of the "terrific twos," "tremendous threes," "fabulous fours," and "fantastic fives." How would you like somebody to say you're in the "terrible thirties" or the "awful fifties"? How we interpret what others say about us and our own self-talk is enormously important because it affects our self-worth, our self-image.

How many times does an executive in the company send out a salesperson saying, "Now handle this one with kid gloves. This is our biggest account. Don't blow the deal." Instead it's much better to say, "We're sending you out because your experience and your skills tell me that you are the only person to take care of this one in the proper way." Give people something to live up to—not something to live down. Visuals and words can pick you up or put you down.

> # WE NEED TO START LOOKING AT CHANGING THE PICTURE WE HAVE IN OUR MINDS OF OURSELVES.

Some people have a picture in their minds of themselves that's so narrow and so shallow that it bears no resemblance to who they really are. A lot of people don't have a clue as to what is available for them. They think others can get this or that or earn this or that, but for them, no way. They have no idea what they *can do* because they've always been told what they *can't* do. And the bottom line is, they have low expectations and because of that they have low results. They have a picture of themselves that is only partially correct.

Again, just having ability and intelligence is not necessarily the key—but *recognizing* that ability, *confessing* it as we claim the qualities, *appreciating* it, *developing* it, and then *using* it, that is the key.

We need to start looking at changing the picture we have in our minds of ourselves. Dr. Joyce Brothers said simply this,

"You cannot consistently perform in a manner which is inconsistent with the way you see yourself." The picture in your mind's eye is incredibly important.

In his book, *Rising above the Crowd,* Brian L. Harbour tells a story of young Ben Hooper who was born in the hills of East Tennessee. Because he didn't know who his father was he was ostracized, treated horribly. Parents wouldn't allow their children to play with him. At six years of age, he was in the first grade. When time came for recess, the other kids would go out and play together. Little Ben stayed at his desk and studied because the kids wouldn't play with him. At lunch he took his little sack lunch and ate by himself while the other kids ate all together. He had a horrible childhood.

> **HOPE IS WHAT CHANGES PEOPLE. ENCOURAGEMENT IS THE FUEL ON WHICH THAT HOPE RUNS.**

When he was twelve, a new preacher came to the small church and Ben heard that he was a loving and wonderful man. Ben had never attended church before, but one Sunday he decided to go. For the first time in that child's life, hope reared its head. Now hope is what changes people. Encouragement is the fuel on which that hope runs. The next Sunday he was there again, and again for five or six Sundays in a row. On the sixth or seventh Sunday, the message was so powerful, so fascinating, so appropriate for little Ben that he didn't even notice that a number of people had come in and sat down behind him. He forgot all about the time and then the message ended and Ben stood up expecting to run out as he had in past Sundays, but this time there were people in the aisles.

He was trying to work his way through when he felt a hand on his shoulder. He turned and looked up and there was the young minister with his hand on his shoulder. He asked him a question which had been on the mind of every person in town for the past twelve years, "Whose boy are you?" People were talking but all of a sudden it got deathly quiet. Then the minister slowly started to smile. His smile spread until it broke into a huge grin and he exclaimed, "Oh! I know whose boy you are. Why the family resemblance is unmistakable. You are a child of God!" And with that he patted him on the back and said, "That's quite an inheritance you have there, boy. Now go and see to it that you live up to it."

Many years later, little Ben Hooper said that was the day he was elected governor of the state of Tennessee and later reelected. You see he had gone from being the child of an unknown father to being the child of the King. And every facet of his life radically, dramatically changed.

ROLE MODELS

I want to talk about one of the finest role models in America. His name is Truett Cathy, the founder of Chick-fil-A. He scratched his way to the top and now the company is worth billions of dollars. Cathy is famous for helping young people succeed in life through scholarships and other youth-support programs. His organization gives millions of dollars to help young people attend college. Cathy was one of the true-blue men who lived his life according to all of the principles that would make anybody successful. Cathy said, "Nearly every moment of every day we have the opportunity to give something to someone else—our time, our love, our resources. I have always found more joy in giving when I didn't expect anything in return."

What a great role model. He lived a scandal-free life, was a wonderful family man, and he and his wife were married sixty-five years. He is a classic example of keeping your life in perspective, in balance. Because of his spiritual dimension and principles in which he operated, he was a significantly successful man who left an admirable legacy that his family is carrying on today. His view from the top, I'll guarantee you, is absolutely beautiful.

Also in the business world, two of my favorite role models have been Mary Kay Ash and Mary Crowley. These two ladies were phenomenally successful in business—both are strongly committed to doing the right thing always. Mary Kay started Mary Kay Cosmetics after she had "retired" from another company. She retired primarily because the owners had, in her opinion, not dealt fairly with people in the organization. As a result, Mary Kay retired. But after about three days, she started putting together a plan so that women would have a tremendous financial opportunity as well as career opportunities, and it would be a run on the principle of putting God first, then families, and then Mary Kay third. The results speak quite well as it became a worldwide, multibillion-dollar company.

My other favorite person is Mary Crowley who founded Home Interiors and Gifts. She contributed literally millions of dollars to Christian colleges for scholarships and helped a lot of people. She taught leadership principles out of the book of Proverbs and held seminars in places that enabled her to relate to women and work with them. She was an enormously successful person. At the twenty-five-year anniversary, in 1983, of the business, her company had achieved $400 million in sales and profits estimated in excess of $20 million. By the early 1990s, sales exceeded $850 million. She and Mary Kay Ash contributed tremendously to all of society and served as excellent examples of having good business principles while applying the Golden Rule in the process.

Norm Miller is another classic example of the fact that good guys really do win! He is head of Interstate Batteries and donates a lot of money to worthy causes. He contributes heavily to missionary causes, church causes, to the homeless and the needy. What he says is what he does—he's consistent, well-balanced, with a beautiful family. He has good standing in the community and is faithful in his services to the church. In 2017, Interstate Batteries celebrated selling a record 18 million batteries in a single year. Although revenue in 2013 was cited to be $1.5 billion, the company is based on purpose and values, stating that, "With our values as a framework, we believe that profits will never drive our success the way our purpose can."

Another classic example of somebody who has a wonderful view from the top is Kurt Warner, former quarterback for the

St. Louis Rams, New York Giants, and Arizona Cardinals. He was an outstanding athlete and is a very wealthy man with a rags-to-riches story. He is significant because he contributes so much to others, especially children, through his First Things First Foundation that he and his wife established.

> THE GOOD GUYS AND THE GOOD GALS WHO HAVE VALUES, QUALITIES, CHARACTER, AND WHO ACHIEVE SIGNIFICANCE BECAUSE THEY DO SIGNIFICANT THINGS— THESE PEOPLE DO FINISH FIRST.

Another favorite person in the world of athletics whom I know quite well is Dennis Parker. Another classic example that the good guys and the good gals who have values, qualities, character, and who achieve significance because they do significant things— these people *do* finish first. Dennis went over to Marshall High where the team had not won a playoff game since 1949. Three years later, Dennis had them in the playoffs, and the fourth year he had them as state champions.

Dennis Parker said to me on several occasions, "You know, Zig, I've never had a young man come back to me after graduation and say, 'You know, Coach, when you taught me how to throw that pass, it changed my life forever.' But I've had a lot of guys come back and say, 'You know, Coach, you remember the story you told me about what happens when you do the right thing? Coach, that changed my life."

These are role models. These are men and women on a mission. These are people on a mission. And because they do so much for others, they themselves end up as the biggest winners of all. And their view from the top is something they enjoy every single day.

CHAPTER 5

FREEDOM TO SUCCEED

You're at the top when you recognize, confess, develop, and use your God-given physical, mental, and spiritual abilities to the glory of God and for the benefit of mankind.

I vividly remember the lady who called in to me on a talk show and she cried, "Mr. Ziglar, I'm fifty-three years old and I've never done anything in my life and now it's too late. It's all over." And I said, "Excuse me, ma'am, how old did you say you are?" She said, "I'm fifty-three and it's too late." I said, "Miss, you're a spring chicken! Does your mama know where you are?"

When she started laughing, her mind sprang open and she was then free to listen with an open mind to what I had to say. Some people are very narrow-minded and believe they have no freedom to see beyond their current circumstances.

For the person who has hit the wall that surrounds them, the first thing I advise is to pick up a good joke book. Look at or read something that is absolutely hilarious, or watch something on television that's very funny. If you have hit the wall and feel as if you can't move forward, you'd be amazed at what laughing will do for your attitude. You need to remember that though you have succeeded in one area of your life, the fun part comes when you succeed in the other parts of life as well. Maybe you've made it financially—that shows you have drive, ambition, direction, and have met that goal. But now you need to look at meeting the other goals in your life, for balance.

> IF YOU HAVE HIT THE WALL AND FEEL AS IF YOU CAN'T MOVE FORWARD, YOU'D BE AMAZED AT WHAT LAUGHING WILL DO FOR YOUR ATTITUDE.

So what's the first step you take? Remember what you read previously—that your physical health is more dependent on your relationships than even the food you eat, your exercise program, and even the genes you inherited. Relationships are so important to so many facets of your life.

For example, concentrate on courting your mate and making amends to your children, if you have any. Maybe you've neglected them over the years. I have seen relationships over a period of time take some incredible, positive turns as a result of simple attention. There are two things everybody wants—to be respected and appreciated. You'll be amazed how much good it will do when you start telling your spouse how much you appreciate all he or she has been doing for you over the years. Tell your children and grandchildren that you are proud of them for what they stand for and what they are doing. Communication is so important—conversation and developing a sense of intimacy will free you and your family of any blockages that may have built up.

FORGIVENESS

Another factor that tends to build up is a degree of resentment. Maybe you've tried to be successful but something is holding you back. Bitterness and anger will hold you back. You'll never be happy as long as you're bitter and angry. Now that may sound foolish, but it's more often true than false. It would be perfectly natural for you to at least temporarily feel that way if you have been abused or neglected. But if somebody has abused you and you've not forgiven the person, that person is running your life. You are bound by that person, he or she has control over you; you have no freedom.

Now think about it for a moment. If they abused you in any way or neglected you, they had a negative impact on your past—and they are negatively impacting your present, at this moment. Now surely you're not going to give them permission to negatively impact your future.

Years ago I gave this talk in Detroit, Michigan, and I went into detail about the value of forgiveness. A young man heard me say that as long as you carry that resentment, you will never have any peace of mind. But the thing that really got to him was when I said, "One of these days you will either say about forgiveness, 'I wish I had' or 'I'm glad I did.'"

The young man told me, "What you said sprang open my mind. When you first started talking about forgiving, I thought that what my dad did to me was too horrible. He doesn't deserve to be forgiven. But when you said that forgiving the other person is for *my* benefit, it made me wonder. And if I couldn't forgive for their benefit, it would be for my benefit. Then you said that the amazing thing is both of us will come out winners. Well, I thought about that.

"I hadn't spoken to my father in years and I went to see him. I didn't want to talk to him on the telephone. When I accused him of what he had done, he denied it completely. He had blocked it out of his mind. I just looked at my dad and said, 'Dad, I want you to know that you did it, but, Dad, I want you to also know two things. First of all, I forgive you. And second, I love you.'"

And the young man looked at me and continued, "Mr. Ziglar, when I said that, he broke down and wept like a baby. Though our relationship isn't perfect yet, it gets closer every time we get together. My father's a relatively young man. Now he can enjoy his grandchildren."

If you've hit the wall, look at all the areas of your life. Look at your friends, your family, all of your relationships. Forgive whoever needs forgiveness, if humanly possible. Commit to following the Golden Rule and the idea that you can have everything in life you want, not just money, but everything in life you want if you just help enough other people get what they want. Concentrate on them. That will take you to a place where you will really be able to enjoy the view from the top.

> ## LOOK AT YOUR FRIENDS, YOUR FAMILY, ALL OF YOUR RELATIONSHIPS. FORGIVE WHOEVER NEEDS FORGIVENESS, IF HUMANLY POSSIBLE.

EVERYTHING YOU WANT

For fifteen years I was in direct sales in the cookware business, showing the cookware through cooking demonstrations. After several years, I finally realized I needed help and ran an ad in a newspaper. All I wanted was somebody to do all of the work. I wanted somebody to go buy the groceries, get the vegetables ready to be cooked, to cook the meal, serve it, and then wash the dishes and the cookware. That's all I wanted them to do. Ha!

Well, a very quiet lady named Jerry responded to the ad. She had been earning money by taking in sewing and baking cakes. When I told her what I wanted her to do, she said, "I love to cook and I don't mind washing dishes. I'll be happy to work with you under the condition that I can't start work with you until after 4 o'clock in the afternoon and that under no circumstances will you require me to participate in the actual demonstration in front of the people. You can tell I'm shy and quiet."

I graciously agreed to accept her terms and things went wonderfully well for a couple of months. Then one night I said, "Jerry, I want you to deliver the cookware I have sold to the people. Take it to their homes and show them how to use the cookware."

Sheer terror came into her eyes. She literally started to shake and said, "I can't do it. I can't do it. I can't teach ladies how to cook on their stoves." I said, "But Jerry, every night for the last two months that's what you've been doing. Isn't it?

"Yeah. But you're always here and I know you'll bail me out if I foul it up. I'm not going to do it. I just can't do it."

Fortunately, we had about a thirty-mile ride back to her home and I guess she got to thinking about it. Just before she got out, she shook her finger in my face and said, "Yeah, I'll do it. But if you ever do this again, I'm gonna let you have it. I'll not get a wink of sleep tonight. And I'm sure I'll do a miserable job." Well I don't know if she slept that night or not; I know I didn't.

The next night about 10 o'clock, I got the most exciting phone call. For twenty minutes Jerry gave me every detail of what happened when she delivered the cookware to the first couple. She told me excitedly, "They had a cup of coffee and a piece of cake waiting for me...and, Zig, I had a wonderful time. And when I got ready to leave, they thanked me profusely and invited me to come back and bring my girls. And they said the next time they'll do the cooking! And they closed by saying, 'Jerry, you have such a beautiful personality and you're so professional.'"

I so regret that I did not keep that customer's name and address because those words literally transformed her life totally and completely. The shy, cake-baking seamstress became one of the most highly motivated enthusiastic people I've ever known. It didn't happen that day, that week, that month, or even that year, but less than five years later, Jerry Arrowwood was a vice president in charge of training for a multimillion-dollar company.

She found the courage it took to make that delivery. It took commitment. She had compassion. She knew that if the merchandise was not delivered the next day, it would affect my reputation. Now I am absolutely certain that when Jerry made the decision to do it, she wasn't thinking that she always wanted to be a vice president in charge of sales training of a multimillion-dollar company. She wasn't thinking, I can have everything I want in life if I just help enough other people get what they want. I'm absolutely certain that did not go through her mind. But what did go through her mind was how I was depending on her and it would be the right thing to do a wonderful favor for me.

She extended a helping hand at a time that it was needed, and when you go through life with that attitude, other good things happen. She got there with one set of values and they were all good, but when she used those values then other values and skills and talents were added. It started with courage, because I'm absolutely certain that she was frightened to death until she made that first delivery. I'd be willing to bet she ran to the second one and the third one. Her fire was lit that night and she kept the fuel on that fire and it kept on burning. Delivering that cookware was not in her job description. But it's true that *when you do more than you're paid to do, you will eventually be paid more for what you do.* Jerry developed into a real optimistic, caring positive thinker and skilled speaker and trainer because she took what she already had and put it to work and the rest developed because she was free of self-imposed limitations.

Wow!

In July 1972, I boarded a flight from Dallas going to Norfolk, Virginia. I was the first one to board. A few moments later, a mother entered carrying an infant, leading a toddler, and a little girl about four years old followed. The little four-year-old stopped to watch personnel loading the food and she was fascinated. Then she turned and looked into the cockpit and saw the pilot and two others sitting there and more electronic gadgetry, in all probability, than she had seen in her entire lifetime. When she turned around, as the saying goes, her eyes were as big as saucers.

It was obvious that this family was taking their first ride on an airplane. The little girl turned again and looked down the long, long aisle and said, "Wow!" That's what legal immigrants do when they come to America. They see the beauty of their surroundings and everything that is here, and that's one of the reasons legal immigrants are four times as likely to become millionaires in America as are people who were born here. They come here with a dream. They know everybody here is rich and that they can become rich and they wake up to new experiences.

Many immigrants look at ads in the paper and see jobs that pay six dollars an hour and it blows their minds. *Man, that's more than I made in six days at home!* They work hard. They work overtime. They enroll in the community colleges. They *do* things and amazing things happen.

When is the last time you looked at your mate and said, "Wow!" When is the last time you looked at your child and said, "Wow!" Or your mom or dad? When is the last time you looked at a sunset or a sunrise and said, "Wow!" It demonstrates an attitude that makes a difference in life. It will make a difference in your life. Let me simply say that this is one of the most important things that we can do—*never lose the awe of the new day.* Your impact on others can be very, very significant.

Let me tell you about a friend of mine. His name is Lou Holtz. Chances are you've already heard of him. He was a football coach—one of the best in the country. Lou was fired from his first job at the University of South Carolina. Now let me tell you something about Lou Holtz when he was at the University of Arkansas. He adopted the philosophy that you can have everything in life you want if you just help enough other people get what they want.

Now here's the way it works in coaching. A lot of people don't realize it, but when he was at Notre Dame eleven years, he promoted ten head coaches from his assistant coaches. Now you might say, wait a minute, weren't they his best assistant coaches? Absolutely. That's the reason they got the offer to become head coaches. Well that's good for the coaches, but what does it do for Lou? How does he get what he wants out of it? Well, an interesting thing happened after the second Notre Dame coach was promoted to head coach of another team. Assistant coaches all over the country heard that Lou Holtz was teaching assistant coaches how to be head coaches and they started applying in droves to coach at Notre Dame. Lou was able to replace his good coaches with sometimes even better coaches.

And he got a bonus. Those new coaches brought all of their high school contacts with them. The philosophy really does work.

NEVER LOSE THE AWE OF THE NEW DAY.

Pursue Opportunity

Now let's start looking at what this philosophy is really all about.

One time when I got into a cab in Mobile, Alabama, I met the driver who was from Nigeria. I have a great interest in immigrants, so I asked him how long he'd been in America. He said twelve years. I asked him if he had been going to school and taking advantage of everything here in the United States. He said, "Absolutely! As a matter of fact, I get my PhD in just two more months, and my wife already has her Master's degree."

I said, "That's great! Do you have any children?"

"Yes, we have four. Their ages are four, six, eight, and ten years and those who are in school are all on the honor roll." I asked him how he's been able to raise a family and get an education all in twelve years.

He said, "As you can see, I'm driving a cab right now. I've also loaded and unloaded trucks. I've been a night watchman. I've been in security. I've been a tutor. I've done whatever it took to accomplish the objective. And I want you to know that my wife has worked fully as hard as I have been working all of this time."

"After you receive your PhD in a couple of months," I said, "then what's the game plan?"

"Well, I've already signed a contract with a major Wall Street firm. My doctorate is in business and finance. I've got a two-year contract with them, and then I go back to Nigeria where I have a prominent position in the government waiting for me."

Now I want you to take a moment to think of the story I just told you. Can you imagine in twelve years what he and his wife had to go through? The number of days they would come home dead tired but there were the needs of the children to take care of—the number of times their bodies cried for sleep? But they had a dream, a vision—they wanted more.

I said, "Where did you get the motivation to do all of this? That's remarkable!"

"When I went to school my first day in Nigeria and came home and asked my parents to help me with my homework, for the first time I learned they were illiterate. They couldn't teach me." He said they were horribly embarrassed. "That day, when I was less than six years old, I decided I would get an education. I never wanted to see one of my children with the expression on their face like I had on my face when my parents told me that they could not help me learn how to read."

To be all that you can be, you need a dream, commitment, courage, and discipline. And then that formula leads to freedom.

FREEDOM OR SLAVERY

For a number of years, a lot of people were singing about being free. In many cases what they meant was—I want to be free to do whatever I want to do when I want to do it and the way I want to do it. Well, many times that attitude actually leads to slavery. *When you exercise your freedom to express yourself at the lowest level, you ultimately condemn yourself to live at that level.*

You're free to experiment with drugs and alcohol, but a certain percentage of the people who experiment with those things end up being slaves to them. Freedom according to the dictionary means exemption from power or control by another. You're free in our society to indulge in smoking and drinking, and as a practical matter, illegal drugs and virtually every immoral behavior. The choice is yours. But that choice all too often becomes a habit and then an addiction, which means, at that point, you've given up your freedom and have chosen slavery.

Pythagoras said, "No man is free who cannot command himself." Gandhi said, "It is my stern conviction that no man loses his freedom except through his own weakness." Charles Kingsley said, "There are two freedoms: the false, where a man is free to do what he likes; the true, where a man is free to do what he ought." The Bible says, "You shall know the truth and the truth will set you free."

Will Durant, the noted historian, said, "Have we too much freedom? Have we so long ridiculed authority in the family, discipline in education, rules in art, decency in conduct and law of the state that our liberation has brought us close to chaos in the family and the school, in morals, arts, ideas, and government? We forgot to make ourselves intelligent when we made ourselves free."

> **A VIEW FROM THE TOP GIVES YOU THE FREEDOM TO BE YOUR VERY BEST SELF, TO MAKE THE MOST CONTRIBUTIONS TO OTHERS WHILE ENJOYING A RICHER, FULLER LIFE YOURSELF.**

Those are really some mouthfuls of wisdom about freedom. A view from the top gives you the freedom to be your very best self, to make the most contributions to others while enjoying a richer, fuller life yourself. Free to learn the new things that will make a difference. Free to be kind and generous and nice to other people. Free to use your abilities to accomplish objectives that are worthwhile that will mean much to you, to society, your friends, family, and to our nation. I sometimes think we forget the incredible price our founders paid to give us the freedom in this country that we enjoy.

But the reality is, if we abuse the freedom and don't use it to become the best we can be, the day will definitely come when we will lose all freedom we have. A study was done by a British anthropologist who studied civilizations spanning over 3,000 years. He found that in 100 percent of the cases when those civilizations failed, it was because they abused the freedoms they had. The family values deteriorated, society turned to immoral ways of living, and crime abounded—as a result, the civilizations failed. Freedom is our most priceless possession.

Remember, we are a nation of laws, not of people. When we follow those laws, we have the freedom to become the best we can be. That's when we will really enjoy our freedom because our view from the top will be so magnificent.

> DISCIPLINE IS THE REFINING PART
> OF OUR FORMULA THAT MAKES
> EVERYTHING ELSE COME INTO PLAY—
> IT MAKES IT HAPPEN FOR YOU.

DISCIPLINE

Wal-Mart founder Sam Walton said, "I think I overcame every single one of my personal shortcomings by the sheer passion I brought to my work." It took courage for that cab driver to leave his native Nigeria in search of education and opportunity. It was more difficult than we can imagine. Discipline is so incredibly important, yet so many people misunderstand discipline. I love what Sybil Stanton said: "True discipline isn't on your back needling you with imperatives. It's at your side nudging you with incentives." How true that is. Discipline is the refining part of our formula that makes everything else come into play—it makes it happen for you.

A lot of people say they don't like the idea of discipline. And I know people rebel against discipline. But think about it in this way—discipline and punishment are two entirely different things. Punishment is what you do when discipline fails. Discipline is a reward. It rewards you for what you have done. Think about it like this. The sailor reaches the desired destination when disciplined to be obedient to the compass. People who have objectives, who have a destination, who discipline themselves will get the things they want. You can have the things you want and more than you've ever dreamed of—but much of it depends on your commitment and discipline and the courage to follow through.

IMAGINATION

A lot of people say that the United States of America is the most powerful nation in the world, and I'm not going to argue with that. But I am going to build a case here for an *imagination* because there is incredible power there. And I want to get you excited about developing and using your dreams and your imagination.

I want to get you as excited as Little Johnny, a second grader. One Friday afternoon the teacher said, "Class, if anything exciting happens over the weekend, tell us about it on Monday morning." So, Monday morning Little Johnny was seated in his desk but he looked very excited. The teacher said, "Johnny, it looks like you had a good weekend."

"Yes ma'am, it was exciting. Me and my daddy went fishin' and we caught seventy-five catfish and they all weighed seventy-five pounds!"

"Now, Johnny, you know that simply is not true."

"Oh yes ma'am it is. My dad is a great fisherman and I'm even better than he is. We caught seventy-five catfish they all weighed seventy-five pounds," said Johnny.

The teacher said, "Now, Johnny. If I were to tell you that on the way to school this morning, about two blocks from here, out of nowhere a big old ten-foot grizzly bear weighing about a thousand pounds rose up right in front of me, was about to grab me and eat me up when a little old eight-pound yellow dog jumped up and grabbed that grizzly bear by the nose, threw him down backward, broke his neck and killed him; Johnny, if I told you that would you believe it?"

He said, "Oh yes, ma'am! As a matter of fact, that's my dog!"

That's how excited I want to get you about your imagination and your dreams and how you can impact so many other people—and in the process make incredible progress yourself. It takes both for it really to happen. Give yourself the freedom to use your imagination and dream.

CHAPTER 6

GROWING YOUR DREAMS

You're at the top when you know a win doesn't make you and failure doesn't break you.

Y ou run your day by the clock, as demonstrated by the day before vacation, but you run your life with a *vision*. You have to have dreams.

When Helen Keller was asked what it felt like to be blind, she said it was much better to have no sight than to have no vision. Solomon said, "My people perish for lack of vision." Albert Schweitzer, the great missionary doctor in Africa, when asked how he was doing, he said, "My sight grows dim, but my vision is clearer than ever."

We need to have dreams; we need to have vision. Walt Disney didn't see a mouse, he saw millions of kids of all ages enjoying his presentations. He built an empire. Neil Rubenstein served as president of Harvard University from 1991 to 2001. His mother was a part-time waitress and his father was a prison guard. But as a young boy, Neil made a very astute observation—that there is a direct correlation between performance and reward. So as a youngster, he determined that the way he could perform better is to have a better education. And despite what his parents were doing, whom he loved very much, he wanted to do more with his life. So he set higher objectives. You absolutely have to have dreams.

I love what Thoreau said, "If one advances confidently in the direction of his dreams, and endeavors to live the life which he has imagined, he will meet with a success unexpected in common hours. If you build castles in the air, your work need not be lost; that is where they should be. Now put the foundations under them." Why don't more people dream bigger?

I believe the story of "Gentleman Jim Corbett," heavyweight boxing champion of the world, has a great deal to say. He was doing roadwork one morning when he spotted a fisherman who was being very successful. He was pulling in big fish and little fish; every time he cast out he would make a catch. But Corbett noticed that the fisherman would take the big ones and throw them back in. He would keep the little ones and put them in his creel. Well that puzzled him so Corbett ran over to him and said, "Sir, I'm a fisherman myself, but I've never seen a fisherman throw the big ones back. I want to know why you are doing that."

The fisherman sadly shook his head and said, "Man, I hate to do it, but I don't have any choice. You see, all I've got at home is a little bitty fryin' pan." Now don't laugh, because he's talking about you and me. We have the big dream, the big idea, but no sooner do we catch the vision than we think, *Oh no, Lord, this is too big when all I got is just a little bitty frying pan. Give me a little one so I don't have to struggle so much. Besides, if that idea was any good, somebody else would already have thought about it. Give me the little one, let me stay comfortable. Don't get me out of my comfort zone.*

Well, I want to get you out of that comfort zone. I want you to clearly understand that you can make some changes; you can build dreams; but again let me say, you make radical changes in small steps.

ONE WORD AT A TIME

At age thirty-seven, Vince Robert was driving a taxi; he only finished the seventh grade. Now where do you think his career and his life were going? Many people would say he would probably end up on welfare or somebody else would support him. Well, one day Vince Robert, while waiting for a fare at the airport or at a hotel where he spent hours every day doing exactly that, suddenly was hit with a bolt-of-lightning thought. He went to a bookstore and bought a twenty-pound Webster's dictionary. He placed the dictionary on the front seat of his taxi and starting on page one, word one, he began to memorize the dictionary. Before he reached an eighth of an inch deep into the dictionary, he noticed something—he was understanding things like never before.

A Georgetown Medical School study discovered that in 100 percent of the cases, with no exception, when your vocabulary increases, your IQ also increases. He started understanding; as a result, he took every dime he could spare and invested in the stock market. When he got dividends, he'd reinvest it. Over a period of time, he bought the nineteen-car cab company and became a very wealthy man.

A couple of things you need to understand about Vince Robert's story. Number one, he didn't start investing one day and buy the cab company the next day. Number two, he *gave up some things he wanted then,* like fancy clothes, a fancy apartment, and fancy automobiles. He gave up what he wanted then in order *to get the things he really wanted later on.* It's called discipline, commitment, responsibility, maturity. The bottom line is he ended up a wealthy man. Now how did he do it? Learning one word at a time, investing one dollar at a time. *Radical change, radical improvement, radical growth—in managed steps.*

I was presenting a seminar several years ago in Dallas, Texas. I was speaking about self-image and self-worth. When the seminar was over, a young woman came up to me incredibly excited. She said, "Mr. Ziglar, what you said today meant a lot to me. My father was forced into retirement a few months ago. He's healthy. He didn't want to retire. He loved what he was doing and wanted to keep on working. But they had that deadline— he was sixty-five. It's all over then. You know what bureaucracy is? An inept group of disorganized people totally committed to the concept of dramatically increasing their numbers so they can more effectively convert pure raw energy to solid waste.

"Well, as a result of his retirement, my father has really become difficult to live with. He's always complaining about this, that, and the other. And in a few months, he and mom are moving to Dallas. I was at my wits' end as to what I could do to help him. I didn't have a clue. And then I looked at the list of ideas you gave me today and now I can help him!"

I looked over the list she had written and there was not one single item listed that I had even hinted about in my talk! What happened? It's very clear and very simple. She knew a whole lot about her dad and she loved her dad a great deal. She knew a whole lot about life as the result of her lifetime of experience. What she did was add new information to what she already knew. Consequently, *the more new stuff you learn, the more valuable what you already know becomes.*

Here's where the *imagination* comes into the picture. The old information, in essence, in the cerebral popped up. The new information popped up. The old looked at the new and started a conversation and said, "You know, if we got together, we could probably create something fabulous!" That's exactly what happened.

That's the reason we need to learn every day of our lives. We receive more than one hundred times as many letters from people saying my books and tapes changed their lives as we do from people who say my seminar or speech changed their lives. Why is that? Using the time in your car going back and forth to your job can make a huge difference. Several years ago, I was a visiting scholar for two years at the University of Southern California. While I was there, they were doing a study and found that if you live in a metropolitan area and drive 12,000 miles a year, in three years' time, you can acquire the equivalent of two years of college education—in your automobile. "Automobile University!"

Twelve years ago, I sold this idea to a young man named Steven Payne, a Cherokee Indian from Bartlesville, Oklahoma. In the ensuing years, he enrolled big time in automobile university. He earned his GED when he was twenty-two years of age. And today Stephen Payne is a translator for his company in both Spanish and French. He also speaks fluent Italian, Japanese, German, Russian, Portuguese, and Norwegian. He's currently learning Cherokee and he's starting to learn Polish as well. Stephen tells me that he learned over 90 percent of it in automobile university.

Don't just sit there to get there; you want to get there better prepared than you were when you left home. And when you leave your job, you don't want to just sit there to get there. You want to get there better prepared to be a good husband, good wife, good mother, good father when you get there. I never give advice that I don't take myself. All the way to recordings and seminars, I listen to tapes myself and almost always pick up an invaluable idea or illustration that's going to help me in what I do.

MORE VALUABLE, MORE CREATIVE

New information added to old knowledge makes you more valuable and more creative. In my own life, I enjoy spending time with that beautiful red-headed wife of mine, I enjoy my exercise program, and I enjoy playing golf. Now to get to do those things,

I've got to utilize my time. I don't consider watching television the best utilization of my time; that is truly identified as an income suppressant. It is also an enjoy-life suppressant. So I do very little of that. I do watch educational programs, but I am generally reading and doing other things.

I read a lot. I've read an average of nearly three hours a day for the past thirty years. I never go anywhere without something to read. If I have an appointment for lunch at 12 o'clock, I take a little book or tear out a magazine article that interests me and I put it in my pocket. I'm going to be on time, but the other person might not be. When I go to the dentist, I know the dentist is going to be working on me about twenty minutes, so I spend the other forty minutes reading something that I want to know.

When I go to the airport and everyone is waiting, I don't just sit there and complain about how crowded airport is—what good does that do? Rather, I'm reading, learning something. It keeps me sharp and it keeps my attitude right. But more important than even those two things, it increases my creativity. Again, the more you learn, the more valuable you are going to be.

DREAMS

My first dream was to buy the used car owned by Fred Shirley who was the rural mail carrier in the small town where I grew up in Mississippi. I was going to get that little car, was going to be at the Chevrolet dealership when he traded it in. And when I got my one-week vacation I was going to get in that little car and I was going to drive that sucker as far as I could in three days. Then I was going to turn it around and drive it back three days because I wanted to be in church on Sunday—my momma would require that, and I wanted to anyhow. That was my first dream.

My second dream was that I was going to run a meat market, because a man who owned the market in town told me he'd help me get started and that he made over $5,000 the year before. Now in the 1940s, that was a whole bunch of money. And then I got the idea that I wanted to get into the Naval Air Corps. My dream was to join. Now the odds were twenty to one that I was going to make it.

I fought the odds. I got in and as a result they started me in college. The war ended; had it not, I would never have seen the inside of a college.

How did I happen to make it? Because of my first-grade teacher. She came to teach me when I was at home with an illness and had to miss four months of school. She taught me my lessons, brought me up to speed, and gave me my assignments. Had she not done that, I would have failed the first grade. I would have been drafted right out of high school into World War II. I never would have joined in the Air Corps. I never would have seen the inside of a college.

And I would not have realized my dream after that dream, which was to be number one in sales, when I started in that career field.

Now my dream today is very modest. I want to be the difference-maker in the personal, family, and professional lives of enough people to make a positive difference in the world. Pretty presumptuous, most people would say. Yes, but the amazing thing about modern technology is that we can go all around the world immediately. My words have been translated into thirty-eight languages and dialects and we've sold more than six million books and millions of cassette tapes—we're making that dream a reality.

> ## NOW YOU DON'T NEED TO START WITH A BIG DREAM BUT YOU NEED TO START WITH A DREAM.

A Dream Foundation

When you have your dream, you need to build a foundation on it. T.E. Lawrence puts it this way: "All men dream, but not equally. Those who dream by night in the dusty recesses of their minds, wake up in the day to find it was vanity; but the dreamers of the day are dangerous men, for they may act on their dreams with open eyes, to make them possible." Now you don't need to start with a big dream but you need to start with a dream.

Ben Feldman is recognized as undoubtedly the greatest life insurance salesman who ever lived. He lived in a huge metropolis in Liverpool, Ohio. As a beginning salesperson, he was struggling to survive by selling $5,000 policies. Then one day he had a little dream and decided to add one more zero to the number—and instead of concentrating on $5,000 policies, he started talking about $50,000 policies. And his dream came true. Then he had another dream of selling policies with one more zero—$500,000 policies. And he did. He dreamed about adding another zero and he started selling half a million-dollar insurance policies in one day—and then $5 million insurance policies—and he did!

Then one day he said, "Suppose I'd dream the impossible dream. Suppose I add one more zero." And he sold $50 million insurance policies. *Dreams grow as you grow.* That's the reason growth becomes so enormously important.

Martin Luther King, Jr. put it this way—*never give up on a dream just because of the length of time it will take to accomplish it.* The time will pass away anyway. Dreams are important. Why don't more people realize it?

I lost weight years ago and kept it off. But I've noticed literally hundreds and hundreds of people whom I've come to know who get on a diet and exercise program and get so excited. They would tell all their friends, relatives, and complete strangers about how good they felt and how great it was to be alive. But I'd see them two years later and they've got no enthusiasm, no zest—and the weight is back. That puzzled me for a long time but then one day I learned about a study, when I was listening in automobile university, done by Stanford University and here's what it said: Ninety-five percent of the people who hear, understand, and agree with a principle do not have the ability to apply it to their lives because they do not have the necessary resources.

Books, tapes, and seminars are the resources. But tomorrow's traffic jams will drown out a lot of what you hear today. Tomorrow's problems that we encounter in everyday life will eat away at much of the emotion that is there when we're so excited about a new venture. Why do I put so much emphasis on automobile university? Because it keeps you fueled; it's food for the brain. Remember seeing the amusing Energizer bunny ads on television? He keeps going and going and going. He runs on batteries and those batteries eventually *will* run down.

ACTION PLAN

But we human beings have a battery between our ears, identified as the brain or the mind, that does *not* run down if you keep feeding it. That is one of my objectives. Always when I talk with people, whether directly or indirectly, my objective is to get them to take action. When you are finished reading this book, if all you say is, "Well, that was nice; I have a good, warm feeling"—then I have not met my objective. After all, you can get a good, warm feeling by taking a bath. Let me encourage you to understand—unless you follow through with action, you will be disappointed in yourself.

> ## UNLESS YOU FOLLOW THROUGH WITH ACTION, YOU WILL BE DISAPPOINTED IN YOURSELF.

What is an action plan and why is it important? Let me illustrate its importance with a true story. When I was a young sales manager, I came up with a little idea. I asked my salespeople to write me a letter every day. Because we lose so much time and we don't know where we lose it, I encouraged them to keep a journal and send it to me. For instance: "Rose this morning at 6:30 and then I…" and they listed the next and next things they did. They discovered that there are about three hours in five, ten, fifteen, and twenty-minute segments when people do absolutely nothing.

As a result of keeping track of activities throughout the day, those who followed through on their action plan sold over twice as much as those who did not. It's an absolute fact that people who go on eating and exercise programs, if they keep a record on a daily basis of what they ate and what they did, they will lose weight faster and keep it off longer.

It's as true for salespeople as for people who want to lose weight. It's true for everybody who wants to climb the stairway to the top. Just remember, the most difficult thing to do is get out of the crowd at the bottom. You start getting out of that crowd when you start taking action with a journal. If you will journal every day, write down what you did, the impact you've had on other people, how you can improve what you're doing, the feelings you get when you encourage and help someone else, how pleased or satisfied you are with your day's efforts—you will rise to the top.

I talk about the day before vacation and how people the world over get more done on that day because the night before the day before, people plan what they're going to do on that last day before vacation. Not only do you plan what you're going to do that day, but you also need to have an action plan for each day. That way you're in charge of your own life, and you can accomplish so much more.

I can't say it too strongly. You need to journal; you need to keep records of your time. There's no need to be long-winded, just simply write the significant points, citing particularly when you received encouragement *from* someone and when you gave encouragement *to* someone.

The next step in the action plan is to write your definition of success based on what you've been reading in this book and based on how you move from here to there and achieve significance in the process. Thinking along those lines, consider this question: If I die tomorrow, would this definition of success leave me feeling my life was a success? You might think that's a pretty heavy question if you're just twenty-five years of age. Well, my friend, it is an established fact that all of us are going to die. So think about it in this serious vein:

If I die today, would I have any regrets?

- Would you have any regrets about the life you have lived and the things you've accomplished?

- Have you really met your objectives?

- Are you on your way to achieving the objectives that you set out?

- When you achieve these objectives that you have defined as being successful, would it really fit all the criteria?

Examine yourself carefully:

- Are you happy?

- Are you healthy?

- Are you at least reasonably prosperous and secure?

- Do you have friends and peace of mind and good family relationships and the hope that the future is going to be even better?

- Do you love people and are you loved?

When you can say yes to those questions, then, my friend, I would be able to say to you that yes you really have achieved significance. It means very simply that you must touch all the bases. You must touch the physical, mental, and spiritual if you you're going to achieve complete success. You've got to deal with your personal life, your family life, and your business life. Yes, your financial life is going to figure in there, too.

When you look at the overall plan, you'll notice this little thing called synergy—that when you put it all together, they work together. Your life is in harmony. That's when good things happen. That's when you've achieved significance—that's when you'll enjoy your view from the top.

> **YOU MUST TOUCH THE PHYSICAL, MENTAL, AND SPIRITUAL IF YOU YOU'RE GOING TO ACHIEVE COMPLETE SUCCESS.**

CHAPTER 7

IMAGINATION AND MOTIVATION

You're at the top when you understand that others can give you pleasure but genuine happiness comes when you do things for others.

It's always been amazing to me to discover that a lot of people think that just because they do not have a corporate job they can't make any difference in people's lives. They only talk about the boring things they have to do. The following are a couple of stories and examples that I believe tie together what you've been learning.

For years I've been saying it's what you do *off* the job that's going to determine how far you go *on* the job. The way you behave during those other sixteen hours is very important. Are you taking care of yourself physically, mentally, and spiritually? Are you making certain that your family is in the game plan with you? Are you learning some things while you're off the job? While you are *off* the job, that's when you learn the things that will make you more effective *on* the job.

If you really don't like the job you have, what about the man in charge of that job? What would keep you from getting the education, experience, and guidance that would enable you to move up the ladder? That's a factor you absolutely must consider.

As an example, I get so irritated with some of the highly paid athletes and television and movie stars when they belittle what they call "hamburger flippers" who work at some of the stands where they play ball, or whatever. On the other hand, I'm excited about those hamburger flippers and all of the employees of the fast-food industry. First of all, they learn dependability, they have to show up on time. They learn how to treat their customers with courtesy and respect. They learn how to operate some of the high-tech machinery. They learn how to develop a pleasing personality. They learn what it is to have their own money. And they treat their own money quite different from when their parents hand them money.

But the rest of that story is that a lot of them qualify to win a new car, win college scholarships, and many of them move up the ladder. I know personally young men and women who are twenty-two or twenty-three years of age who drive luxury automobiles by flipping those hamburgers. They are now managers earning $50,000 to even $80,000 a year. *It doesn't matter where you start, that's not important. Where you go is what's significant.* And I don't care what the job is, when you take the approach of doing something off the job to improve yourself, then you will either move up in the one or you will get a better offer from someone else.

> ## IT DOESN'T MATTER WHERE YOU START, THAT'S NOT IMPORTANT. WHERE YOU GO IS WHAT'S SIGNIFICANT.

I was raised during the Depression and in those days, inventories were small because dollars were so tight. The grocery stores literally loaned each other their food such as canned food items. I was a "runner." When the store would run short because they hadn't bought enough because the owner didn't have enough money, I would run to other stores and borrow what we needed. At another grocery store, a young man named Charlie worked there as a runner. He would run into our store many, many times and tell the owner what he needed. While Charlie would go get the items, the owner would write out the receipt. Charlie would scribble his name on it and take off running. One day I asked the boss why Charlie ran so much and he said, "He's working on getting a raise—and he's going to get it!"

"Really?" I said. "How do you know he's going to get a raise?"

"Well," said my boss, "I know he's going to get a raise because if the man he's working for doesn't give it to him, I'm going to hire him and give it to him."

Many years later when I was speaking at Mississippi State University, I told that story and when the seminar ended, a man came up to me—it was Charlie. Because he maintained that habit of working hard and giving his absolute best every day, he was able to retire at age fifty-five as a very wealthy man. After retirement, he contributed all of his time to charitable causes and helping other people achieve success.

My friend, I don't care where you start, you can still achieve significance. You can still enjoy the view from the top.

MOTIVATION

I love the story of two skiers. They were almost even during the competition—one was just an eyelash ahead of the other. Then one skier fell. So the other one thought she'd be the first one over the finish line. But then she fell too. The skier who fell first came down the hill and won. Someone said to the loser, "That's too bad you didn't win, she was faster." She said, "No, that's not it. She wasn't faster—she just got up faster." That's what makes the difference.

To get knocked down is part of life. How long you stay down is determined by how committed you are and how energized you are. That's why it's so important to keep learning new information all the time. A dream is more certain and more easily realized if life is in balance. If we worry about what's going on at home and then when we get home if we're worried about what's going on at the office, we're not doing a good job in either place. Our life is not in balance. The bottom line is we have a lot of difficulties—and troubles will be solved more quickly if life is balanced.

> TO GET KNOCKED DOWN IS PART OF LIFE. HOW LONG YOU STAY DOWN IS DETERMINED BY HOW COMMITTED YOU ARE AND HOW ENERGIZED YOU ARE.

My wife and I have a balanced relationship. What makes that relationship balanced? First of all, you put the other person first. Second, do something for your wife or your husband every day that they can do for themselves. Two simple little things. In the nearly fifty-five years we've been married, and in the two years, two months, and eleven days we courted, she has not opened her car door a dozen times. Every time I walk around the car and open the door, I'm reminded that here is the most important person on the face of this earth to me. Here's the one I love above all those little things that pop up to grab my attention.

Years ago I stopped carrying my money in a wallet. I'd just fold it over and put it in my pocket. At night I'd put it on the bathroom counter. She started counting my money, and if she didn't think I had enough to cover unexpected expenses on my next trip out of town, she would always go get me some more. Now that's not a big deal, but what it says is everything. It says, "Honey, I love you very much. You're extremely important to me. I will feel better knowing that if there is an emergency and you need cash, you will not be embarrassed, delayed, or perhaps even endangered." Putting the other person first makes a huge difference.

My wife is known affectionately as The Happy Hugger. If it's moving, she will stop it and hug it. If it is not moving, she will dust it off and sell it. We average hugging somewhere between ten and up to thirty times in a day to simply say, *I'm so glad you're mine and I love you very much. You're special.* I can't begin to tell you what it meant to me to have her beside me during those first twenty-seven years of our marriage. We had our telephone disconnected, lights turned off, had to turn a car back in because I couldn't pay for it. When our first baby was born, we couldn't even get her out of the hospital—the bill was $64. I had to go out and make two sales so we could bring our baby home. During one five-year stretch, I was in seventeen different deals, and that's all they were. None panned out.

During all those years, not one time did my wife ever say, "Honey, you know it would be nice if we had more money. It would be wonderful if we had a little more stability in our financial situation." She never said anything like that. She always said, "You can do it. Tomorrow is going to be better. I love you and I believe in you." I can't begin to tell you what it meant to me to have a cheerleader cheering me on every day of my life and praying for me every night.

You would not be reading this book if it had not been for the fact that we were on the same page. She bought the dream of me doing what I'm doing now. I had my dream in 1952, but it was 1972 before my speaking career exploded. That's a long time, and I needed lots of help along the way.

We need to understand why balance is so crucial. Consider this fact: if all the gold in the world were melted down into a solid cube, it would be about the size of an eight-room house. But all those billions of dollars could not buy a true friend, character, peace of mind, a clear conscience, or a sense of eternity.

GROUNDED IN THE BASICS

How do you develop the imagination that makes all of these things happen? Number one, you need to ground yourself in the fundamentals of your chosen profession. For example, Asian math students do infinitely better than American math students when they get to advanced math. They are better because they're so grounded in the fundamentals. For example, you can wake up the Asian math student at 3 o'clock in the morning and ask, "What is seventeen times twenty-three?" And bang, the student spits out the answer to you. They're so grounded in the fundamentals that when they get in the abstract, it's easy.

Michael Jordan is recognized as one of the greatest basketball players who ever lived. He makes shots that nobody else has ever made. Why can he do that? To begin with, he has great athleticism, there's no denying that. It's an absolute fact, he is a remarkable athlete. But also we need to understand that he was one of the hardest workers at practice. He dribbles magnificently well. He passes behind his back, between his legs, and finds himself in different positions and every situation is different. He never has exactly the same score with exactly the same teammates and exactly the same opportunities at the same time of the game. He's always faced different opportunities.

This is where his athleticism and his imagination and his dream come into play. He makes those moves and there's nothing but net. Fundamentals and grounding are the principles I'm talking about; constant learning is what makes the difference. Thomas Edison is famous for the fact that he had to experiment several thousand times to finally invent the light bulb. Shortly thereafter, Edison was approached by a reporter who asked, "How does it feel to have failed thousands of times in this process?" Edison replied, "Young man, I didn't fail thousands of times. I successfully completed those experiments and learned what did not work."

He added new information to the old knowledge and that's how he produced the electric light bulb.

That's so important. I have a lot of medical doctor friends, and they tell me that 95 percent of all the problems they will ever encounter as doctors, they learn in the first three years of medical school. And yet they attend for another year and then they go in specialization and they continue to get upgraded. But they really could solve 95 percent of the problems with a third-year medical education. When they continue, they want to be able to figure out how to treat the three-in-a-million cases that come along. That's where the imagination, built upon all of the experiments and all of the knowledge they have, comes into play. Those are the great doctors who come up with creative solutions.

DESTRUCTIVE HABITS

A chance remark sometimes triggers your imagination and you will come up with ideas if you are really tuned in to your goal. I eat, sleep, and dream teaching and speaking. My objective is simply to encourage and lift up other people. So, everything I see or read or hear, in most cases, I can take it and use it as an application. For example, the last time I got a haircut, my barber, Bob, who has been cutting my hair for over thirty years, received a phone call. He picked it up and after about a minute conversation, he put the phone down and said, "That guy wants to work for me; but he smokes, and I'm not going to hire him."

I said, "I'm glad of that. I don't want to come for a haircut and leave smelling like smoke."

Bob said, "Oh, he wouldn't smoke in the shop. But the problem with a smoker is the fact that if he wants to smoke but there's somebody in his chair, his mind is outside smoking a cigarette, not on the customer's haircut. I want somebody who will concentrate all of their time on the people they're supposed to be serving."

What use is that conversation to me? For years I've been interested in learning about addictions. And what I've discovered is that people who are addicted are inclined very strongly to become self-centered. You will seldom find somebody with a serious addiction who does not have serious relationship difficulties. The relationships we build make us more effective—if we do not have a destructive habit that takes our attention away from our project.

Imagination can also be very destructive. In the twenty-four years I was overweight, I lost a couple thousand pounds. I'd go up and down and up and down—losing and gaining weight for twenty-four years. I finally figured out my problem when my youngest daughter was just a little three-year-old and I told her to call me "fat boy." It didn't matter how much weight I lost, I had to completely change the picture I had in my mind about myself. My three-year-old thought she was pleasing her daddy; I thought it was funny. Later I realized it was tragic.

So what did I do? I began a sensible eating and exercise program; but I had done that before. But this time I put up a picture of a trim guy in Jockey shorts. When I went into the bathroom every morning and saw that dude, I said it a thousand times a day: "That's the way I'm gonna look! I going to look just like that guy." I changed the picture in my mind and that was thirty years ago. I am a healthy, slender person brought about because I dreamed that I was going to be that way.

My imagination went to work—and I took the steps that made it happen. I lost those thirty-seven pounds by losing one and nine-tenths ounces a day, on average, every day for ten months. The weight is still gone. Today I eat everything I want without a problem. Now one of the things I've discovered along the way is that if I did without sugar, the rest of it was extraordinarily easy. So, I quit eating sugar—no cookies, cakes, ice cream. I'm a sweetaholic, but there are many things I want to do and I need to be healthy to do them. I want to be active all of my life, if it's humanly possible. I want to go out full speed ahead, wide-open doing everything I can possibly do. *Using your imagination makes a difference.*

DREAMS COMES TRUE

My dream to be a speaker was born in 1952 after hearing a presenter. I never saw a man have so much fun and do so much good as that speaker, and that night I made the decision to be a speaker. My wife and I cornered him after the seminar and took him to dinner. Remember, it's very important to allow other people to teach us. He told me some steps I needed to take, and from that night on, the dream was in my mind.

During the following years before I ever got a single paid engagement, I had made literally thousands of speeches—in my own mind. I saw myself in front of an audience. I saw people sitting there in wide-eyed astonishment that a mere mortal could utter such incredible words of wisdom. When I told a joke, not only would they laugh, they would roll up and down the aisles. They had never seen or heard anything like what I said.

The beautiful thing about your imagination is that you can take it anywhere you want to go. That's the reason I keep saying to *make certain the input is positive so the picture is positive so the results will be positive.* And the time came when my dream became a reality and then my career absolutely exploded. Your imagination is so important. Your dreams are so important.

I met a young man when he and I were speaking for the Department of Defense in Colorado Springs a number of years ago. There were CEOs of Fortune 500 companies, the Secretary of Defense, and more brass than I had ever seen in my life. John, a college student, stood up and spoke with authority and conviction. We became friends and I've been working with him in his speaking career. He speaks all over the world, skis, is a portrait painter, drives his own car, lives in a three-story house, scrambles his own eggs—and the reason I mention those things is because he was born without arms.

John said to me on time, "You know, if I had the longest, strongest arms in existence, they still could only reach so high and lift so much. But every day of my life I encounter more situations where I have to use my creative imagination than the average person encounters in a month. God has balanced it all out."

And here's the interesting part—something so small spurred something so great. His parents were dismayed when their son was born. They wondered: What on earth can he do? What will we be able to do? How can we help him? One day they noticed something exceptional. When he was less than a year old—about eight to ten months of age—he was sitting on a table and beside him was a toothpick. He reached out with his toes, picked up the toothpick, dipped it in the sugar bowl, and put it in his mouth. His parents were ecstatic! Hope was born in that moment. They believed that if this child can do all of those things at this age, he can learn how to do so many other things. A dream for him was born. And then John inherited that dream.

Why is imagination important and how do you develop one? You keep learning and keep studying, you keep listening, you keep following through. When you get a big dream, instead of saying, "no way," say, "I can do it" and start exploring the ways that you can accomplish it.

> WHEN YOU GET A BIG DREAM, INSTEAD OF SAYING, "NO WAY," SAY, "I CAN DO IT" AND START EXPLORING THE WAYS THAT YOU CAN ACCOMPLISH IT.

YOUR BEST SHOT

I have a book called *Secrets of Closing the Sale.* There is one segment in that book titled "The Heart of the Sale" and it has seventy-one pages. I've been selling since I was eight years of age. I sold newspapers, vegetables, and so forth on the streets of my hometown in Mississippi. Because I've been selling and training almost all my life, I had a huge backlog of information on selling when I wrote the book. Remember, the more prepared you are, the more grounded you are in what you do, and the more valuable new information becomes.

I encourage you to learn your profession. Whatever your choice is, learn every single thing you can about it. People who don't believe in dreams will say, "Hey, this person really knows what he or she is talking about!" I do a lot of speaking and I talk about the same things a lot. I've given the same talk several hundred times around the world. When I spoke to Hewlett Packard I used 90 percent of the material that I have used hundreds and hundreds of times before. Of course, I customized it to their needs and wove that information in to make it applicable to exactly what they do. Beforehand, I spent an hour on the telephone with them getting what their objective for me was.

For a regular public seminar presentation that I've made hundreds of times, I still spend from three to five hours preparing for that talk. Now why do I do that? Number one, I think it's arrogant for a speaker to stand up and say, "Well, I've done this so many times I can spit it out. No problem." I go over it because there's a great deal at stake. We have a responsibility in whatever we do to give it our absolute best. I leave absolutely nothing lying on the table because I know that one day I will give my last talk. I don't want to look back and think that I could have done it better. Although I'm not always at my best—I always try to give my best.

The sweetest sleep on earth is when you can lie down at night after you've looked yourself in the mirror and said, "Today I gave it my best shot." God has given us so much—ability, experience, opportunity—and you need to capitalize on those gifts with your dreams and with your imagination, with your commitment and your courage. You need to put it all together and use that information to the benefit of others, clearly understanding that you really can have everything in life you want—if you just help enough other people get what they want. You'll have lots of friends; you can end up being happier and healthier, more prosperous, more secure, have more freedom and greater peace of mind—and the hope that the future is going to be even better.

> ## WE HAVE A RESPONSIBILITY IN WHATEVER WE DO TO GIVE IT OUR ABSOLUTE BEST.

If you do all of these things, you'll not only love but you'll be loved, because you are the right kind of person doing the right thing—and your view from the top is going to get better all the time. Act on your ideas and dreams because when you do, I will definitely be able to say to you, "Welcome to the top! The view is magnificent...and look at all the people you brought with you!"

And you will smile and say, "I've had a rich and full life."

CHAPTER 8

YOUR
MISSION IN LIFE

You're at the top when you've made friends of your adversaries and have gained the love and respect of those who know you best.

The mission we have in life is enormously important. Undoubtedly, it is the most important thing that we can do in our lifetime. Over the years, millions of people have done some remarkable things without a mission statement—in fact, that phrase wasn't even known until relatively recently. It is important to really explore what is your mission in life, what you really want, and determine what is important to you.

My own mission has changed over a period of years. But the new mission statement our business has adopted has allowed things to happen in a much more effective and significant way. *Our mission is to be the difference maker in the personal, family, and professional lives of enough people to make a positive difference in the world.* That's a pretty significant mission statement. It's actually a little presumptuous.

At the time we put this mission statement into practice, we were much smaller and had far fewer works—books, tapes, etc.—out in the field. But since then, as mentioned previously, our works have been translated into thirty-eight different languages and dialects, we've sold over six million books, and I've spoken to roughly six million people in large audiences. Plus, I have no earthly way of knowing just how many people have listened to the tapes other people have bought and shared. We are reaching people worldwide—and now through the internet, we're able to go into numerous other countries with our messages of hope and excitement and enthusiasm.

When you have that big picture cited in a mission statement, you can start painting in the spaces that will enable you to be more comfortable, more confident, more productive, and more effective—doing a lot more good for a lot more people. The mission should challenge you. It should take you toward a significant role in life. It should be something that you believe in fervently; and you don't just have a mission, the mission has you.

Think of a man like Dr. Billy Graham. Most everybody recognizes that name. His mission was identified early on and he was absolutely true and committed to that mission until the day he died at the age of ninety-nine. Although his health deteriorated over the last years, every time he got up to fulfill his mission to preach the gospel, there was a new strength and new power in his messages. Toward the end, he almost had to be helped to the platform, yet there was power in his voice. He had a mission—and the mission had him.

IDENTIFYING YOUR MISSION

To identify your mission, think in terms of your natural talents. What do you enjoy doing? In what do you believe fervently? What is something that you just can't keep your mouth shut about? You have to talk about it, think about it, write about it. When a subject meets those qualifications, then you will begin to realize what your mission in life is.

Don't be discouraged if you can't put in writing exactly what you're feeling the first time around. When we worked on our mission statement, not only did I work on it but several of our key staff members did too. We would brainstorm by asking questions such as: What is the mission? What does it mean? How will we be able to accomplish it? We were more interested initially in identifying the mission, then we drew the game plan for accomplishing the mission. That's the process we went through and we're following today.

One idea propels another; one accomplishment enthuses us and convinces us to take the next step now.

And you need to take that first step. You need to get pen and paper. You need to start thinking quietly about what you want to do. What is your mission? You can think about it while you're taking a walk, in the quietness of your mind and heart. You can explore it as you arise in the morning and when you go to bed at night. When you do it this way, discovering your mission becomes absolutely critical to you and passion grabs you. When passion grabs you as your mission begins to unfold in your mind and you can articulate it, it becomes real in your mind.

> WHEN YOU PUT ALL OF THE COMPONENTS OF YOUR MISSION TOGETHER, THERE WILL BE A NEW EXCITEMENT, A NEW COMMITMENT, AND A NEW CONVICTION IN YOUR LIFE.

Once your mission is established and the mission statement put together, then you need to start examining each area of your life. Ask yourself:

- Can I do this consistently in my personal life, my family life, my professional life?

- Will this work in the physical, the mental, and the spiritual aspects of my life?

- What will be the financial results?

Finances are important. Finances are one of the factors in many divorces; there are so many disputes over money. We need to have a game plan to answer all those questions to eliminate any kind of destructive circumstance.

When you put all of the components of your mission together, there will be a new excitement, a new commitment, and a new conviction in your life; consequently, you can put your whole heart into it. That's important! After a high jumper broke a world record, somebody asked him how he did it. He said, "It was really quite simple. I threw my heart over the bar and the rest of me followed." Put your heart in it—the rest of you will follow, and then you will achieve significance in your life. Your mission statement is critically important. Put it together. Then you can say you know the view from the top really is beautiful.

YOUR EULOGY

One good way to get started on your mission statement is to answer the question: What do you want your eulogy to be? If you can put that together in your mind, you will have taken a significant step toward defining what your mission is.

I would like whoever is delivering my eulogy to say, "Zig would not change anything." Years ago, I heard a lady say something that made a lot of sense to me and I borrowed it for my own. She was asked what she would change if she had to or could live her life over. She said, "I wouldn't change anything, because if I'd changed anything, I would not be where I am. And I really like where I am." Those are my sentiments exactly. Although I've made many, many mistakes, all of them were part of the plan for my life. If I change anything, I might not be where I am and, like I say, I really do like where I am.

The reason I can say that is because I truly know where I'm going when I breathe my last here on earth. I truly have given my very best shot. I've taken the abilities God gave me and I've worked very hard at utilizing, developing, improving, and improvising those abilities. I can honestly tell you I love my family and my fellow man. I have done my very best to make a positive contribution to society by doing what is right—understanding that other people are critically important not only to the success of any endeavor, but also to our enjoyment of life, our happiness, and our joy.

I wouldn't change a thing. I believe people want to be treated with respect and dignity. They want somebody they can look up to—not somebody who will look down on them. I believe that's what a eulogy should contain. That's what I want mine to contain.

I believe when you have your eulogy put together, you will be pleased with what you've written. Not only that, but the eulogy will serve as a benchmark and a guideline for your life. It will make a difference in your life. It's serious, but this stuff will make a difference in your life not only in the future but in your eternal future. That's what significance is about, and that's what the view from the top is about.

The mission statement you put together should be so simple, direct, and brief that anyone can memorize it in a matter of minutes. The specificity in your mission statement should be a guideline that enables you to develop the plan of action to complete or fulfill the mission. It should be so clear and so distinct that it guides you toward the direction you need to take and the plans you need to put together to make that mission statement viable.

It should be something you can get excited about and you can say to your friends and your family, "This is my mission statement and I want to put together a game plan to make it happen." You might even want to talk to them during the process and ask them what they think your strengths are and maybe they can suggest possibilities.

> ## WHAT DO YOU WANT YOUR EULOGY TO BE?

MENTORS

This is where mentoring comes in. This is where somebody whom you trust and respect can be of help to you. In my life I've had twenty-six people who had a huge impact on my life. They're on my wall of gratitude. But at the moment, I have one mentor with whom I share everything. He always has something significant to add to me and to whatever I'm doing. He's a wise man, a knowledgeable man, and he's very interested in what I do. Find someone like that to guide you along when writing your mission statement. It might be a pastor, a rabbi, your next-door neighbor, a former employer, or former schoolteacher. Anyone you can trust to share what's burning in your heart.

First, you need to set yourself on fire about your mission, then the world will gather to watch you burn with excitement that will take you toward the destination you have identified in the mission statement. It's a good and proven process to follow.

One of the things I want to make crystal clear is the fact that you can have a mission without having a mission statement. I refer to my mother, for example, a person who had a huge impact on my life. She only finished the fifth grade, but she had incredible wisdom. One simple example of that wisdom follows. I went to work in a grocery store on the Saturday before I entered the fifth grade. I worked fifteen hours for the grand total of seventy-five cents. This was back in the Depression years, so that was not uncommon.

I'd been working at the grocery store for three years when I got an offer from a sandwich shop where I was going to be paid $1.15 a day. At the grocery store job, I went to work at 7 o'clock in the morning and got off at 11 o'clock that night. At the sandwich store I would have gone to work at 10 o'clock in the morning and gotten off at 10 o'clock at night. I would have made forty cents more. That might not sound like a lot but in those days, for a dollar people could buy a twenty-four-pound sack of flour, three pounds of good bacon, and fourteen small oranges. It was a significant amount of money and I wanted to make the change.

But my mother never even considered it. She said to me, "Son, the additional forty cents would be good. But I don't know the owner. He might be a good man, but I have heard they sell beer at that sandwich shop and that's an environment I don't want my boy to be in. I *do* know Mr. Anderson. I know he's a good man, and I know that he will take proper care of you and it is the environment you need to work in." This shows the wisdom of my mother.

Mr. Anderson became more than just an employer. He was a surrogate father. He even took me to a grocery convention in New Orleans, Louisiana. It was the first time I had ever been out of our little town where I was living. On Wednesday afternoons he would take me with him out to his farm and I would watch him as he dealt with the foreman of the farm and the way he dealt with the people there who worked for him. I learned an awful lot about life from my mother, and also from Mr. Anderson. Our son is named John Thomas Ziglar. The John comes from John Anderson, the man for whom I worked in the grocery store, and the Thomas from my wife's father's name.

Now what's this got to do with my mother's mission? She had twelve children. Her commitment was to raise those children in the fear of God and the love of the Lord. She wanted them to be successful in every area of their lives. I heard her say many times, "I only have twelve children and Satan is not going to get any one of them." Every bit of her mission was to make certain that her children were saved and going to go to heaven. Her mission was to give them the best chance in life to have a good life. She knew that honesty, faith, and character were the base on which she could build. No, she didn't put it in writing, but she made her mission in life very, very clear.

BASELINE

Your mission is important—but what role does it play in our lives? Chances are good that you have heard of the Johnson and Johnson company. And you may remember the Tylenol scare here years ago where millions of dollars' worth of that particular medication was available in drugstores and grocery stores all across the country. Johnson and Johnson had nothing to do with the fact that someone with a demented mind had put poison in a couple of big containers of Tylenol. But Johnson and Johnson never hesitated. They took every bottle off the shelves at a cost of many, many millions of dollars. Public confidence not only was restored, but it grew dramatically. Johnson and Johnson has a mission statement based on values, and it's proven that companies who have a written values statement based on character really do win.

> **IT'S PROVEN THAT COMPANIES WHO HAVE A WRITTEN VALUES STATEMENT BASED ON CHARACTER REALLY DO WIN.**

One of the marvelous beauties of having your mission statement is that inevitably you will be confronted with situations where you have to make a decision that you're not comfortable making. As a result, you can go right to the mission statement; and if the decision is contrary to the mission statement, you will know right then you have to do something to correct the decision. That's the way you accomplish your objectives and can be very comfortable with what you have done.

The same is true of individuals. I'm thinking about Gertrude Johnson Williams who had a mission statement. You might not have heard very much about her unless you read her son John Johnson's autobiography. John Johnson's mother and John were born in a tin-roofed house in Arkansas City, Arkansas, and they had a tremendously difficult time in life when John Johnson finished the eighth grade. In those days, African-American kids were not permitted to attend high school, and there was no high school in Arkansas City. So what did Gertrude Johnson do for her son? She made him take the eighth grade over again.

Why did she do that? Because her mission was for him to have the better things in life. She did not want him to be idle, nor did she want him to become accustomed to doing menial jobs. She had a plan to take him and the family to Chicago where they had relatives and where the opportunities would be greater. They worked long and hard. John and his mother did difficult things, everything possible to raise enough money to make the trip to Chicago where they lived with relatives until they could get on their own. They were embarrassed to say they had to be on welfare for a limited period of time. But the bottom line? She had a mission for her son.

Her mission has accomplished great things through her son, including: He founded a number of companies and published *Ebony* magazine. He was the guest of every president in the White House since Eisenhower. He was one of the wealthiest men in America, worth $150 million, when he passed away in 2005. John H. Johnson is famous for making the statement, "It's not the color of your skin, it's not the place of your birth—it's the size of your hope that's going to determine what you do in life." John Johnson had hope because his mother had a mission.

When you have a mission, you will do great things as well. As long as you're faithful to the right mission involving doing things for other people and based on character and integrity and lots of hard work, then you'll enjoy the view from the top.

NATIONAL AND GENERATIONAL MISSIONS

The United States of America was founded because of a mission—people wanted freedom to worship. When the Pilgrims came to America, they were really excited about their mission and the privilege of having freedom to worship. That particular freedom was so important to them—as was the importance of building character and faith in their children. In 1776, there were three million Americans. And of those three million Americans, honorable, creative, courageous, and wise men were raised up, including George Washington, Benjamin Franklin, John Adams, George Washington Carver, Alexander Hamilton, Thomas

Jefferson, and many others. Now the country is currently at 300 million Americans, and it's not as easy to find men and women of character and integrity. I challenge you to name just one person who has the commitment, the accomplishments, the intellect, and the faith that these founders of America had.

Why is that? What happened along the way? According to a research institute, in 1776, having the New England Primer and other works including the Bible, over 90 percent of all of the educational thrust at that time was from a character-based, religious, faith source. By 1926, that percentage had dropped down to just 6 percent. And by 1951, the percentage of character and faith included in the educational process was so small it could not even be measured. Does your character count? Does faith count? Does having the right concept about what life is all about count? Yes. I rest my case on the fact that our great nation was founded on the principles written in the Constitution—that we all have the same rights and privileges.

As I mentioned previously, I'm the tenth of twelve children. Dad died when I was five. I was raised during the Depression. And yet because of the society in which we operate, because of the educational opportunities, the privileges we have, and because we are not judged by the color of our skin or the family we came from, but judged by what we do, we are rewarded as a direct result of having a mission and character and faith—all the things that make huge differences in life. That's why I tell people to get that mission statement so you can build on a solid foundation. That's the best way to get to the top and stay there. Why on earth would you want to go anywhere else when the view from the top is so wonderful?

STABILITY

If you interviewed the average person on the street today, they would tell you that there is so much transition taking place in every area of life. The family is being redefined. Security is being redefined. People move from one place to another more often. The divorce rate is going up. Violence is rampant. There are school shootings, drunken brawls, and the like.

How do we survive in a world like that? How do we achieve any stability? How do we make our lives more meaningful? How can we succeed in this environment? First of all, we need to accept responsibility for our own performance and our own conduct. We can survive and thrive when we have the right base, when we understand that we have to be the right kind of person and do the right thing in order to have all that life has to offer.

We need to remember that what somebody else does should have no bearing on what you do. Just because somebody else lies and cheats and steals and steps out on his or her mate, that certainly is no reason for you to do it. The evidence is completely overwhelming that the good guys and the good gals, the honest ones, are the ones who end up at the end of the road with not only more of the things money will buy, but also all of the things that money won't buy.

What happens down the street should be of concern to you. That's the reason I believe we need to get involved in civic and social clubs, churches, and politics. A lot of people say, "Oh don't get involved in politics. That's a dirty business." Well, if everybody thinks it's a dirty job, guess who's going to get in it—nobody but bad people. If you want to change things for the better, help put the good men and the good women in there. Those who have values, those who have upstanding beliefs, those who have commitment, those who accept responsibility, those who have an interest in other people, those whose word is their bond. That is significance.

> WE NEED TO REMEMBER THAT WHAT SOMEBODY ELSE DOES SHOULD HAVE NO BEARING ON WHAT YOU DO.

TRUST

Trust is the glue that holds society together. When there is no trust in a society, it comes apart. You might wonder what you can do to help build trust. You can first take care of your own needs, then your family's needs, then you can reach down and extend that helping hand to others. I'll never forget what a coach of mine told me when I was in junior college. He said, *"If you have an ability that goes beyond providing for your own needs, you need to reach down and lift up other people."*

The first two and a half years I was in sales, I was not an overwhelming success. That doesn't mean I didn't sell anything, because I did—I had to sell my furniture and my car. But finally after two and a half years, I went to a meeting and a man said some things to me that made a huge difference in my life. He gave me a belief in myself. In those two and a half years I had learned how to get prospects, learned how to make a deal, learned how to conduct demonstrations, learned how to close sales, and learned everything a salesperson is supposed to know. The salesman was ready, but the man was not.

This man looked me in the eye and said, "Zig, if you just believed in yourself and went to work on a regular schedule, you could become the national champion." After that, I didn't quite make it, but out of 7,000 salespeople, I did finish number two. That year, everything I touched turned to gold. I was selling like you cannot believe. I remember vividly, though, the second phase of the story that completely changed my life. The heavy-duty waterless cookware company I worked for had a national booster week. During this week we were to concentrate all of our efforts strictly on selling—no collections, no training, no nothing but sales, sales, sales. That week I ended up selling two and a half times as much as I'd ever sold in a week.

My wife and daughter went to Jackson, Mississippi, that week. That's where she was from. They wanted me to work real hard that week—and work hard I did. On the way to pick them up and bring them home after that great week, I stopped in Atlanta, Georgia, about 2:30 in the morning for a break from driving. I awakened a good friend and mentor of mine who put on the coffeepot. For the next two hours he listened to every word

I said. I told him about every call I made plus gave him every detail. When I finally finished, I apologized for talking so long and so much and asked him how he was doing.

He said, "Zig, don't give it a thought. You have every reason to be proud of what you've done." Then he reminded me that he was the one who recruited me for the business and kept me encouraged, inspired, and trained. He was the one who talked to me when I threatened to quit. Then he said, "Zig, as excited as you are about what you've done, you will never know what joy is until you have experienced what I have just experienced. When someone you have trained and shared yourself with turns around and succeeds—that's what joy is all about."

My friend, that's what having a mission is all about. If your mission is to do well yourself, but more importantly to teach others do well and help them to do well, then you will have accomplished real significance. That means you will be totally enjoying the view from the top.

In summation, number one, you need to write your mission statement and you need to start working on it this very minute. Number two, you need to develop a plan of action in order to accomplish your mission. Number three, you need to make your mission a reality by considering the people you need to talk with or work with to do some brainstorming. Number four, you need to make the commitment to follow through so that not only will you reach and fulfill your mission statement, but as a result of you reaching the mission that you set forth in that statement, you will help other people so they too can enjoy the view from the top.

As part of your action plan for this mission and mission statement, you need to write it in a journal or notebook. You need to make copies of it and post it so other people can see it so they know what your mission statement is. They need to be part of the mission in order for it to be fulfilled. When you take these steps, things will happen; but until you put them into action, they are simply empty words that will take nobody anywhere. Follow through. That's the way you enjoy the view from the top—because that's where you will be.

CHAPTER 9

SIGNIFICANCE AND SPIRITUALITY

You're at the top when you're filled with faith, hope, and love and live without anger, greed, guilt, and the thoughts of revenge.

I n our day and age we're hearing more and more talk about spirituality and religion. From my perspective, unless we embrace this spiritual aspect, we miss out on the most significant part of life itself. I'm going to make a statement that you might at first rebel against and disagree with, but here it is: I believe that deep down everybody believes there is a God. There is an old saying that you'll never find an atheist in a foxhole—I believe that is absolutely true. The following information is what leads me to believe that's more than just an old saying.

Back when companies could use a polygraph to determine whether or not to hire a person, for many, many years Brown Trucking Company out of Atlanta, Georgia used that option. Polygraph tests were conducted on thousands of people over a period of years, as they had over 100 facilities throughout the country. Brown Trucking Company reported that in 100 percent of cases, with no exceptions, when the question was asked, "Do you believe there is a God?"—in every case when the person said, "No," the polygraph needle went berserk, indicating that absolutely yes, the person did believe there is a God. This question was asked every time to thousands of prospective employees.

I love the story about an incident in Mordecai Ham's life—a fiery evangelist instrumental in Billy Graham's conversion. Reverend Ham was about to start preaching one night when a gentleman walked up to him and said, "Mr. Ham, I just wanted you to know I've come to hear you tonight out of pure curiosity. I don't believe in God. I don't believe in heaven or hell, and I certainly don't believe in prayer."

And Mordecai Ham said, "You're a very unusual fella."

The young man said, "Well, I just wanted to let you know in advance that's the way I feel."

When it came time for Mordecai Ham to preach, he got up and said to the congregation, "Now folks, we got an unusual fellow with us tonight. He says he doesn't believe in God, doesn't believe in heaven, he doesn't believe in hell, and he said he certainly doesn't believe in prayer. So what I want all us to do right now and during the entire time I'm preaching, I want you to pray that God will kill him."

What happened next? The guy jumped up and ran out screaming, "Don't you do it! Don't you do it! Don't do it!" That man had just proved that he *did* believe in God and he *did* believe in hell, and he *did* believe in prayer!

One of the godliest people I've ever known in my life was widowed with eight children left at home. She lost her husband on a Thursday and the following Tuesday her baby died. This happened during the heart of the Depression. She had a fifth-grade education. Her faith in God is the thing that pulled all of us through—she was my mother. Her life, while it was a very difficult one, had a considerable amount of significance.

I never will forget one little incident that enriched my life and made me determined to be more attentive to everything I did. We went to a family reunion every year and everyone would bring their goodies for the pig out. On average, each person's weight gain was about three and nine tenths pounds. We didn't eat until we got full—we ate until we got tired! Most of the family lived close by our hometown, so they drove. But we had to fly, so we had to buy the food when we arrived that we would be contributing to the gathering. We went to the local grocery store and put into the cart a smoked turkey, smoked ham, and a whole bunch of candies and soft drinks.

When we got to the checkout counter, the cashier gave the bill to my wife. My wife reached into her wallet and pulled out a couple of credit cards and her driver's license to show the cashier because we were from out of state and she was going to write a check to pay for the groceries. But when the cashier saw the name on the check, she said to us. "Around here, the name Ziglar is all the ID we will need."

Now please understand that this was way before I became known—before the books and tapes and speaking engagements. I was absolutely unknown at that time. This woman was talking about a mother who even when she was flat on her back could sign a note from the bank and get a large sum of money because they had learned many, many years ago that when Mrs. Ziglar signed a note, that meant there would be no question about that note being repaid.

That day I renewed a commitment that whether or not I ever left my children a dime—I was going to leave them a good name. When anyone saw their name, they would say this is all the ID we need. My mother accomplished her objectives in life, which was to make certain her children were raised properly and had faith. Those objectives wouldn't have been met if not for the spiritual dimension of her life.

ETHICS AND INTEGRITY

One of the magnificent facts about spirituality, about faith, is the fact that it absolutely changes you for the better. It affects your ethics, values, relationships, and every facet of your life. It affects the way you treat other people. It affects the way you treat your mate, your children. It's the way you handle the truth. Many people in our day and world say, "Well, I just made a mistake." What they are really saying is, "I know I was wrong when I lied about that; it's just a mistake. Now that I've admitted it's a mistake, let's put it behind us and go on."

> **IF YOUR SPIRITUALITY, YOUR FAITH, IS STRONG, IT ENABLES YOU TO LIVE CONSISTENTLY ACCORDING TO ETHICAL AND MORAL STANDARDS.**

In spirituality, you don't just put it behind you and get on with your life. You make restitution. You ask for forgiveness; you take care of the wrong you have done. If your spirituality, your faith, is strong, it enables you to live consistently according to ethical and moral standards. To not live consistently is, of course, hypocrisy. Hypocrisy is one of the heinous things that is looked down on by virtually everybody everywhere. No one likes a hypocrite. To say one thing and do something else is entirely out of character.

One of my biggest disappointments involved two men—which turned out to be an asset for me. This sounds a little strange until I explain it. In the early part of my career, I had experiences with two men who were internationally known and respected. I went into a business relationship with each one of them, and it didn't take me long to realize that what they said and what their public persona was, was entirely different from what they were and what they did in private.

In one particular case, for the first and only time in my life, I became completely discouraged. The man had looked me straight in the eye and lied to me. I mean big time. I invested a great deal of time and a considerable amount of money in building an organization—and it was taken away from me. When I received the telegram announcing that particular decision, I was devastated. For about three weeks I was virtually helpless. I didn't have the energy to do anything. Had I not had a wife and children who were depending on me, I really don't know what would have happened.

I decided that if I ever was able to achieve any degree of notoriety, if I ever became known, the one thing I was going to work the hardest at was being consistent in whatever I did. I wanted to make certain that what anyone saw was what they got. And I'm telling you now, that has been one of my greatest privileges and assets—because over the years that reputation has kept me in good stead.

Your ethics, your integrity, and your very life should be the role model, the example for others. And when you are, people will notice.

One year as we were starting our own company, before it was actually launched, one of the other competing companies called and asked me to speak for them. I had spoken for them many, many times, so I told them frankly, "I'd be happy to speak but you need to know that we are preparing to launch our own company. Of course, I would not talk about what we do, I'd talk about your business, but I want to be upfront about it." The caller's response was very gratifying. He said, "Well, I'll talk it over with a couple of the staff, but we're not worried about you. We've dealt with you for many years and we know you'll do the right thing." That was one of the finest compliments I ever received.

After the talk was over, I received letters saying it was the finest talk I'd ever made for them. They were paying me; I was working for them, so I gave my 100 percent, best effort to them. Ethics make a difference in life—that's consistency, that's integrity, that's spiritual.

People want to know who you are. They want to really know where you're coming from, what kind of person you are. If they see consistency in your life, then they know you can be depended on. If you're consistent in the way you treat others, they know there must be a reason for it. So, the idea of not talking about your spirituality is absurd—just *let your reputation and your character and your integrity shine through.*

> PEOPLE WANT TO KNOW WHO YOU ARE. THEY WANT TO REALLY KNOW WHERE YOU'RE COMING FROM, WHAT KIND OF PERSON YOU ARE. IF THEY SEE CONSISTENCY IN YOUR LIFE, THEN THEY KNOW YOU CAN BE DEPENDED ON.

CONSISTENT

One of the amusing, if it wasn't so tragic, concepts that a lot of people have is that you're not supposed to have any money, you're not supposed to be rich. Even throughout the Bible, it shares about our physical and financial well-being. There is nothing wrong with earning and accumulating wealth—especially if you use it for the purpose of others. This is a wonderful thing. But if you give money just to get the publicity that goes with it, then the gift is of an entirely different nature—it's ego and publicity driven, making it not significant. But when you give it with a sincere heart for the good of others, that's significant. Those are the people who have a marvelous view from the top.

One of the major factors concerning people today is how do we inject into society and share with our children our spiritual values? As my mother told me years ago when our children were young, "Your children pay more attention to what you do than what you say." What we do, people notice. If we are not faithful to the faith, they won't follow the faith. Why should they? Mahatma Gandhi said, "I might have been a Christian—if it hadn't been for Christians." When we are faithful to the faith, they will follow the faith. They will see you are consistently kind and generous, honest and dependable.

In my own spiritual walk, I take a fairly routine approach. I do it because I've found it works for me and it keeps me zeroed in and focused on the target. As I like to tell people, I like to keep the main thing the main thing. When I get up in the morning, 99 percent of the time the first things I do are shave, wash my face, comb my hair, brush my teeth, then I put my clothes on, go downstairs and turn on the coffeepot. I'm an early riser. I generally get up about 5 o'clock.

While the coffee is brewing, it takes about ten minutes, I do my praying. I pray for my friends, my family, those in need, and those sorts of things. I also pray for wisdom and guidance for the day. I pray that God will protect me and my family and that He will give me the right attitude and wisdom to make the right decisions. Then, in my office, I spend about thirty minutes reading my Bible and devotions by various Christian authors. All this prepares me for the day, which I believe gives me a huge start.

We need to have a routine to strengthen our spiritual lives. A lot of people complain about lack of time, but I believe it's a lack of direction that is the big problem. When you make commitments and want to really develop a healthy spiritual life, whatever routine fits in your life, I encourage you to follow through. Now obviously if you have three small children underfoot, you're not going to be able to do the things that I've been doing. That's a different situation.

> A LOT OF PEOPLE COMPLAIN ABOUT LACK OF TIME, BUT I BELIEVE IT'S A LACK OF DIRECTION THAT IS THE BIG PROBLEM.

It might be that the afternoon, when the children are taking a nap, would be a good time for you to do your Bible study. Prayer can be on the top of your list all the time. I do an awful lot of praying throughout the day—when I'm doing just about everything. It's a habit now. Obviously, I pray before each meal because God has blessed us. A lot of people in this world don't have anything to eat every day, so thanking Him for what we have is a good routine that enables you to do that.

Another special routine could well be praying with the children as you're putting them to bed at night. This could be one of the most beautiful spiritual experiences you can possibly imagine. I believe strongly that *the way you start your children's day and the way you end their day will have a dramatic impact on what happens in between those hours.* Remember the way you awakened when your baby was an infant or when the baby cried? You lovingly picked up and held the baby close and talked or cooed. Why not awaken your babies that way all of their lives? For example, instead of going by the door of your eight-year-old and banging on it, yelling, "Get up!" how about gently knocking and then walking in and saying, "It's time to get up" as you tousle his or her hair.

Then you go to the kitchen, turn on the coffeemaker, come back, and again knock on the door.

If you've never done this before, you want to tell them the night before you start that tomorrow there's going to be a little surprise when you wake them up. Then sit on the side of the bed, stroke their hair, lean over, and kiss them on the forehead or the cheek, and say, "You are so beautiful, or handsome, I love you, and I'm so glad God sent you to live with us. Today is going to be such a good one. You're going to have fun. You're going to learn lots of things, and I can't wait until you get home so we can talk about all of the good things you learn today."

Then when bedtime comes, if your child's bedtime is 9 o'clock, at 8 you say, "Okay, it's time to get ready for bed. Remember, in one hour we go to bed. If you need to put the cat out and bring the bicycle in, do it now. Call Sally about the assignment. You need to take both trips to the bathroom and get all three drinks of water, because at exactly 9 o'clock we're going to bed and we're going to have fun when we go."

Then at 9 o'clock you turn the television set off. The ultimate insult to the child is to put them to bed during a commercial. We raised four children and, we believe, successfully. Yet I clearly understand that the greatest con artists walking this earth are between the ages of six and thirteen. They use every device at their disposal including asking incessant silly questions to keep you there as long as possible so they won't have to go to sleep right away. Children are amazing. They resist going to bed with all the fervor at their disposal—then during the night they develop a lifelong romance with the bed. They form a loving attachment to it and you almost can't separate them from it the next morning. That's the way they are.

At bedtime, children talk to keep you there with them. Let them do it. They will get over the silliness in a matter of two or three minutes, but during that time you will bond with your child. Maybe in those next ten minutes you will bond more than you've been able to all day long. They will tell you what's on their heart.

They will ask you serious questions. You can tell them a story or read the Bible, or you can pray with them. That's injecting into their lives what it is to be spiritual in yours. That's the way you share and spread your faith; and in the process, you're raising a child who will have a significant impact in life and the future later on. That's why the view from the top is so beautiful.

FEELING BETTER

We live in a hurry, hurry world. We've got instant everything. There are many people who really don't quite understand that every day is a significant day. Why not start the day more slowly and deliberately instead of awakening at the last moment to the sound of that opportunity clock? Some people call them alarm clocks, but alarms frighten people and opportunities excite people. So why not set that opportunity clock a little earlier so you have time to start your day casually and slowly. It won't hurt you to look at the sunrise every once in a while.

When you start your day slowly, doctors will tell you that's good for your health. Get up early enough to have time with your child. Get up early so you can eat a more leisurely and more complete breakfast. Physicians will tell you in a moment that breakfast is the most important meal of the day. So when you start slowly, pray about your food, thanking God for that food. When your family sees you doing that, when they see you doing the things that you say you believe, then they will know that you really do believe. The simple starting of the day slowly and ending of the day slowly with your family, you'll discover that all of the time in between—when you've invited God to participate—will be a lot smoother.

This ritual is so important—most everything we do is by habit. Once you get in the habit of doing this, you will find it's a routine that enables you to have a more balanced life. You will feel better about yourself and you will feel better about your future. You feel closer to the family, closer to God, and when you put all of it together, you will discover it is the result of having established a habit of following a procedure that produces results.

Eventually, you won't even have to think about doing it. You simply get up each morning and start doing it. Consistency enters your life and spirituality becomes important. It's an approach to life that really makes a difference. That's the way you achieve significance and you will enjoy the view from the top even more.

> ## WE LIVE IN A HURRY, HURRY WORLD. WE'VE GOT INSTANT EVERYTHING. THERE ARE MANY PEOPLE WHO REALLY DON'T QUITE UNDERSTAND THAT EVERY DAY IS A SIGNIFICANT DAY.

CHAPTER 10

BALANCED,
SIGNIFICANT
GOALS

You're at the top *when you made friends with your past, are focused on the present, and optimistic about your future.*

Many people are confused about what it means to have it all. They think, for example, that they can spend twelve hours a day at work and then spend a couple hours in an exercise program, and then play a round of golf. They think they can do all of those things and still come home and be a good husband or a good wife and cook the meals and clean the house and do all those other things that need to be done at home. That reasoning, of course, is absolutely absurd. They're not going to have much of anything when they follow that routine. They won't have good health, they won't be happy, and they won't have virtually any of the things that everybody wants.

> ## IT'S IMPORTANT TO PRIORITIZE, ORGANIZE, MAKE THE COMMITMENT, HAVE THE DREAM, AND KEEP RECORDS.

When I talk about having it all, I have identified the things that constitute *all*—happy, healthy, at least reasonably prosperous and secure, to have friends, peace of mind, good family relationships, and the hope that the future is going to be better. Also the need to love and be loved. Can you have all of those things? Yes. You certainly can. But it starts with that character base mentioned throughout this book. It starts with a dream that you have. And it starts with your organizational process putting all of them in the formula.

I encourage you to consider carefully again what you read about when I described the day before vacation and how all of those things fell into place. Remember, lack of time really is not the problem, it is lack of priorities—that is the problem.

I'm grateful to be able to say that yes, I do have all of those things—but I work at them every day. I do the things that need to be done and I segregate my life to this degree: when I'm at home, I'm really at home with that redhead of mine; when I'm on the job, I'm intense and I concentrate on what I'm doing.

It's important to prioritize, organize, make the commitment, have the dream, and keep records. Keeping track of your plan's progress is so you clearly understand that these things are not going to happen by accident. They are going to happen because you *plan* on them happening and you follow through. That's the reason there's so much motivation in this program—a view from the top. As mentioned earlier, Stanford University's study revealed that 95 percent of all of the people who have an idea never followed through because they did not have the resources.

Right now you are holding in your hand the resource that enables you to have it all. But let me tell you something. If you finish reading and say, "I really enjoyed that book," that would please us. But we're looking for a lot more than that. If you say, "I really got a lot out of that!" that would make us even happier. But when you get through it and say, "I really enjoyed this, I got an awful lot out of it, and here's my game plan, my action plan, that I've put together to make it happen for me," that's the way you have it all.

BALANCED, SIGNIFICANT GOALS PROGRAM

And now we need to look at a balanced, significant goals program because it is an important part of life. Howard Hill was undoubtedly one of the greatest archers who ever lived. He entered

287 archery tournaments and he placed first 287 times. I've seen newsreels of Howard Hill shooting a bull's-eye target dead center and then the next arrow would split the first one down the middle. Incredible. He could outshoot any rifleman in the world from a distance of thirty feet. He was amazing. So, when I make the next statement, you're probably going to raise your eyebrows and think I'm kidding you. I'm not very good at archery myself, but I'm an instructor extraordinaire. Now let me tell you just how good I am. I could spend twenty minutes with you, and if your eyesight is good and your physical health is good, in twenty minutes I would have you hitting the bull's-eye more consistently than Howard could on his best day—provided, of course, we had first blindfolded Howard and turned him around a couple of times so he would have no idea in which direction he was facing.

Now you're thinking, *Obviously, nobody can hit a target they can't see.* That's a good point. But let me make a better one. How on earth can you hit a target if you don't even have one? Do you have a goals program? The benefits are enormous. If you have a goal, did you write it down? And did you:

- Identify the benefits that would be yours when you reached it?

- Identify the difficulties, the barriers that stand between you and getting there?

- Identify what you need to know in order to get there?

- Identify the people, the groups, the organizations you'll need to work with to accomplish it so that it will be significant?

- Develop the exact plan of action?

- Set the date for reaching that goal?

Until you do those things, my friend, you don't really have a goal—you just have a wish or an abstract dream that might, might not, but probably will never take place.

Let me tell you one of the benefits, actually it's a combined benefit, from having a goal program.

There was a UCLA study on the people who attended Peter Lowe's huge success seminars. These people include everybody from psychiatrists, truck drivers, government workers, civil service workers, physicians, college students and professors, household executives, entrepreneurs, CEOs of big companies, CEOs of small companies, and military personnel. Out of all of those people, those who had a balanced goals program earned an average of $7,401 a month. Those *without* a goals program earned an average of $3,397 a month. This has been recorded in academia—there is proof.

But here's the rest of the story. Not only did they earn more than twice as much money—they were happier and healthier and got along better with their family at home.

The reason for that is very simple. When you have a plan of action and know the direction in which you want to go, you simply don't sweat the small stuff; you're able to do so much more when you have a goals program. I encourage you to get heavily involved in following through. The discipline that goes with a goals program is one of the major keys in making it happen. Discipline is so important.

DREAMS AND GOAL-SETTING

The first thing you need to do is write down in a notebook or piece of paper with the heading "Dream Sheet" all the things you ever want to be or do. It should take you about an hour. Then put it aside for twenty-four to forty-eight hours, because during that period of time you will think of other things you want to add to it. This is very important.

After that day or two, you need to ask yourself some questions about each of the things you wrote:

- Is this really my goal?

- Is it morally right and fair to everyone concerned?

- Is it consistent with other goals?

- Can I emotionally commit myself to finish this goal?

- Can I see myself reaching this goal?

- Will reaching this goal make me happier?

- Will reaching this goal make me healthier?

- Will reaching this goal make me more prosperous?

- Will it make me more friends?

- Will it give me peace of mind?

- Will it make me more secure?

- Will it improve my relationships with others?

Now if you can't answer yes to one or two of these questions, just kind of scratch that goal out for the moment. What you need to remember is that you have to have some big goals to cause you to reach and be significant—they may be out of reach right now, but not out of sight. Keep that in mind.

You also need some long-range goals. The reality is, you will have some short-range frustrations and failures; and *if you don't have long-range goals, then every obstacle becomes the whole ocean front.* But when you have a long-range goal, then the obstacle simply becomes a pebble on the beach. Go as far as you can see and then when you get there, you'll be able to see farther.

You also need daily goals. Those are what keep you active. Some goals are ongoing like developing your self-worth, getting a better education, building better relationships with your family, improving your time on the treadmill, etc. There are some things you are always working on. And some goals require consultation like financial goals and educational goals. Most goals must be specific.

When you make those dreams your goals and ask yourself those questions, that long list you started with will be absolutely reduced dramatically, and that's important. You see there are probably more than 50,000 ways in America to earn a living. So, you have to focus on what is important. To reduce the goals, walk down the list, asking yourself, *Is this really my goal?* Go right down the list and you reduce it considerably.

Yes, goals are enormously important. Follow the instructions and discipline yourself to follow through because discipline makes the difference—especially on those days when you flat-out don't feel like doing anything.

> GO AS FAR AS YOU CAN SEE AND THEN WHEN YOU GET THERE, YOU'LL BE ABLE TO SEE FARTHER.

DAILY DISCIPLINE

When I was working on my weight loss and involved in other things as well, I had a speaking engagement in Seattle, Washington. I flew there that morning and flew back that night. By the time I got home and got ready and in bed, it was 4 o'clock in the morning. Now in those days I thought I had to exercise the first thing in the morning so I had set my opportunity clock to get up at 5:30 each morning. Well, as I looked at my clock and thought about getting up at 5:30, I thought, *If I get up at 5:30, I'm going to feel terrible.*

I almost pulled out the plug—I really didn't want to get up when that clock sounded off. I really didn't. I was still grumbling a little bit when I put on my shoes and went for my jog. I surely did not have any fun on that run and the day was not very productive. Yet, that is one of the most important decisions I ever made—to keep my commitment regardless of the circumstances, no exceptions.

Exceptions destroy people's dreams and keep them from being significant. If an alcoholic has been dry for three years but takes just one drink, you know what happens then. If I had given in to my exhaustion that night and didn't get up the next morning, then the next time maybe on four or five hours of sleep I would've thought I could skip my exercise, and so on. It takes discipline to accomplish goals. If you take this approach to life, you are going to enjoy your view from the top.

Self-Talk

In reaching your goals, which is to achieve significance and maintain a balanced life, you need to talk to yourself, big time. I mentioned this earlier in the book when on the subject of your day-before-vacation approach to life and how if you used those qualities daily, good things would happen. You've got a lot more qualities than we identified that day. Photocopy and use the following personal commitment and the following pages which contains a *life-changing procedure*.

GETTING STARTED:
MY PERSONAL COMMITMENT

I, _____ , am serious about setting and reaching my goals in life. So, on this _____ day of 20 ___ , I promise myself that I will follow these suggestions in setting and reaching my goals.

I am willing to forgo temporary pleasures for the pursuit of happiness and to strive for excellence in my goal-seeking efforts. I am willing to discipline my physical and emotional appetites to reach the long-range goals of happiness and accomplishment.

I recognize that to reach my goals I must grow personally and have the right mental attitude, so I promise to specifically increase my knowledge in my chosen field and regularly read positive growth books and magazines. I will also attend lectures and seminars, take courses in personal growth and development, and utilize my time more effectively by listening to motivational and educational recordings. I will keep a list of these activities.

Persistence and commitment are prerequisite to reaching my goals, so I promise I will work faithfully on my goals daily. I agree to chart my progress daily. And I commit myself to reaching the top, where I know I'll enjoy a magnificent view.

Signed: _____

A Life-Changing Procedure

The eyes are the windows of the soul. So, to become the person you are capable of becoming, each evening, just before you go to bed, stand in front of a mirror alone and look yourself in the eye, and in the first person, present tense, repeat with passion and enthusiasm paragraphs A, B, C, and D. Repeat this process every morning and every evening from this day forward. Within one week, you will notice remarkable changes in your life. After 30 days, add the procedure at the bottom of this card.

A. "I _____ , am an honest, intelligent, organized, responsible, committed, teachable person who is sober and loyal, and who clearly understands that regardless of who signs my paycheck, I am self-employed. I am an optimistic, punctual, enthusiastic, goal-setting, smart-working self-starter who is a disciplined, focused, dependable, persistent, positive thinker with great self-control, and I am an energetic and diligent team player and hard worker who appreciates the opportunity my company and the free enterprise system offer me. I am thrifty with my resources and apply common sense to my daily tasks. I take honest pride in my competence, appearance, and manners, and am motivated to be and do my best so that my healthy self-image will remain on solid ground. These are the qualities that enable me to manage myself and help give me employment security in a no-job-security world.

B. "I _____ , am a compassionate, respectful encourager who is a considerate, generous, gentle, patient, caring, sensitive, personable, attentive, fun-loving person. I am a supportive, giving and forgiving, clean, kind, unselfish, affectionate, loving, family-oriented human being, and I am a sincere and open-minded good listener and a good-finder who is trustworthy. These are the qualities that enable me to build good relationships with my associates, neighbors, mate, and family.

C. "I _____ , am a person of integrity, with the faith and wisdom to know what I should do and the courage and convictions to follow through. I have the vision to manage myself and to lead others. I am authoritative, confident, and humbly grateful for the opportunity life offers me. I am fair, flexible, resourceful, creative, knowledgeable, decisive, and an extra-miler with a servant's attitude who communicates well with others. I am a consistent, pragmatic teacher with character and a finely tuned sense of humor. I am an honorable person and am balanced in my personal, family, and business life, and have a passion for being, doing, and learning more today so I can be, do, and have more tomorrow.

D. "These are the qualities of the winner I was born to be, and I am fully committed to developing these marvelous qualities with which I have been entrusted. Tonight I'm going to sleep wonderfully well. I will dream powerful, positive dreams. I will awaken energized and refreshed; tomorrow's going to be magnificent, and my future is unlimited. Recognizing, claiming, and developing these qualities that I already have gives me a legitimate chance to be happier, healthier, more prosperous, and more secure, and to have more friends, greater peace of mind, better family relationships, and legitimate hope that the future will be even better."

Repeat the process the next morning and close by saying:

"These are the qualities of the winner I was born to be, and I will develop and use these qualities to achieve my worthy objectives. Today is a brand-new day, and it's mine to use in a marvelously productive way."

After 30 days, add the next step:

Choose your strongest quality and the one you feel needs the most work. Example: Strongest—honest. Needs most work—organized. On a separate 3x5 card, print *"I, _____ , am a completely honest person, and every day I am getting better and better organized."* Keep this 3x5 card handy and read it out loud at every opportunity for one week. Repeat this process with the second strongest quality and the second one that needs the most work. Do this until you've completed the entire list. Use this self-talk procedure as long as you want to get more of the things money will buy and all of the things money won't buy.

> **Note:** Because of some painful experiences in the past (betrayal, abuse, etc.), there might be a word or two that bring back unpleasant memories (example, discipline). Eliminate the word or substitute another word.

The following stories illustrate the positive results of using these self-talk strategies.

When I first started this project and was deeply involved in the importance of self-talk, there was an occasion in New Orleans that I will never forget. A lady and her daughter were there and I was talking about claiming for yourself the qualities of faith, honesty, integrity, and hard work.

A little over two months later, I received a self-taught card the lady sent me that her daughter had been using. On this card, the daughter had underlined and underscored and started claiming all of the qualities that were there, including the one on faith. The mother said to me in the letter, "Mr. Ziglar, my daughter became a Christian. She was killed on February 27 of this year." I have to tell you that was one of the most moving experiences I've ever had. It demonstrates the power of claiming the qualities that God has put in you. You need to look yourself in the eye, get in front of the mirror, and claim the qualities.

One of the reasons they work is because they are all biblical qualities, simply meaning that they absolutely have been tested and tried over thousands of years.

The second and equally moving experience I've had with self-talk was when I was in Salt Lake City. I had spoken to a large organization and afterward I was signing books when a lady came up and said, "Mr. Ziglar, I need to talk to you." And the look in her eyes told me that I needed to listen, despite the fact that there was a line waiting behind her.

She said, "When I heard you speak and got your tapes and looked at all of those qualities, I got the card. But I have to tell you when I looked, just quietly, at some of the qualities that you wanted me to claim, I could not claim them. No way. I'd been beaten down all my life. There was no way I thought this way about myself. I had to listen to your tapes several times before I could even get through the first two or three statements on the card. I couldn't continue until I listened to those tapes some more."

And then she said, "The day came when I could get down to about eight of those qualities and, Mr. Ziglar, when that happened, for the first time in my life I realized that I had value, that I could do things with my life, that I was important. And I literally sank to my knees and wept with joy and relief. I kept listening. I kept talking. I keep claiming these qualities. I appreciated the fact that you mentioned that despite the fact that I was awfully weak in some of the qualities, in Joel 3:10 it clearly says, 'Let the weak say I am strong.'

"So I kept talking and kept doing the things you were talking about, and after three or four weeks, my husband said to me, 'There must be something to this. I'm seeing a dramatic change in your life and I'm going to do exactly what you are doing.'" Then the lady looked at me, and with tears in her eyes said, "Mr. Ziglar, for the first time in years I believe there's hope not only for me but for our marriage."

There is no joy that equals someone sharing that kind of experience with you. There are so many things you can do that seem small, yet to another person they might be huge. If you keep practicing and talking about the things that you've been reading about in this book, you will become a difference-maker in other people's lives.

Now I'm just going to read a few of these qualities, and you look yourself in the eye and say: "I, _____ (your name), am an honest, intelligent, organized, responsible, committed, teachable person who is sober, loyal, and clearly understands that regardless of who signs my paycheck, I am self-employed. I'm an optimistic, punctual, enthusiastic, goal-setting, smart-working self-starter who is a disciplined, focused, dependable, persistent positive-thinker!"

All of this self-talk gives you self-control. And the reality is, until you learn to manage yourself, you're never going to be able to lead other people. Claim all of these qualities every morning and every night for thirty days. And after that you need to identify two specific qualities you have—number one is the most powerful, the most positive, the strongest quality you have; and number two, identify the weakest quality you have.

Let's say you're an optimistic person but your organizational skills are not strong. What you do next is write on the card and then say out loud, "I am a complete optimist and my organizational skills are getting better and better every day." You're going to discover that something amazing will happen.

I'm sure you've noticed that when you buy a green Ford, all of a sudden everybody in town starts driving green Fords. Likewise, when you absorb these qualities, everywhere you go and everything you do, something intriguing happens. For example, when you turn on the television set, what are they talking about? How to get better organized. You go to a restaurant and sit down for a cup of coffee and the people in the next booth are talking about getting better organized. Newspaper and magazine articles are about how to get better organized.

You will become convinced that there is a conspiracy out there to help you get all of those things in life you want. And you know what, you would be absolutely right. It's amazing what happens when you start moving in this direction. People will step aside, pat you on the back, and say, "Go get 'em!" You'll have encouragement everywhere you go.

DISCIPLINE AND OBEDIENCE

People have asked me, "How long do I keep doing this self-talk?" My answer, "Only as long as you want the benefits...that's how long you keep doing it." It's amazing what happens when you keep the input positive, keep claiming the qualities, and keep following through—and I guarantee you're going to love the view from the top.

One of the reasons that immigrants are so successful, in fact they are four times as likely to become millionaires in the United States as those who are born here, is the fact that they practice a tremendous amount of discipline. I think this story demonstrates exactly what I'm talking about.

I had the privilege of speaking to the Notre Dame football team before one of their bowl games. Before the game, my wife and I were having dinner with Coach Lou Holtz, three assistant coaches, and three student assistants. While eating our meal, about every two minutes, one of the assistant coaches would tell one of the student assistants that he needed to have more information about a specific scenario. Immediately, one of the student assistants would jump up and run to find out whatever needed to be done. Then two minutes later another one would take off, then another—they were up and down and up and down almost the entire time.

Although it was kind of fun to watch, I kind of felt sorry for the guys and gals because they weren't getting much to eat. While they were all gone on one of the trips, the head coach said, "Zig, we have about 250 freshmen students who volunteer to be student assistants. And at the end of four years, out of the 250, about 50 of them are still serving. Occasionally I meet them when travelling around the country and they tell me, 'Coach Holtz, I was a student assistant at Notre Dame for four years.' And I always ask them the same question, 'What is the name of the company you're running today?'"

Lou said that in 100 percent of the cases, they will either name the company or they would say they're not running the company but they have hundreds of people in their department. He said that these young men and women have accomplished much because of the discipline they enforced upon themselves and the spontaneous obedience they offer the person in charge of telling them what to do. There's never a chip on their shoulder or any resentment.

For years I would read where certain military commanders, after twenty years' service, are now CEOs of various companies, and I think to myself, *What on earth can that man or that woman know about running a corporation?* When I started doing work with the military and some of their training programs and creating training programs for them, it finally dawned on me that in the military, the first thing you learn is obedience. When you're on the firing line and the commanding officer or the sergeant says move out, there's no time for debate or hesitation. Obedience is expected and orders are to be followed through—as lives may depend on it someday.

Now as you move up you learn tact and diplomacy about it, but the expectancy is the big key. And that's what Lou Holtz was saying to me about those young men and women who had done so well—they had discipline and obedience in their lives, which are keys to succeed.

> IT'S AMAZING WHAT HAPPENS WHEN YOU KEEP THE INPUT POSITIVE, KEEP CLAIMING THE QUALITIES, AND KEEP FOLLOWING THROUGH—AND I GUARANTEE YOU'RE GOING TO LOVE THE VIEW FROM THE TOP.

Authoritarian
and Authoritative

One of the most important distinctions we need to make if we expect to ever enjoy the view from the top is the difference between authoritarian and authoritative. Authoritarian simply means that a parent says to a child, "Do this because I said do it." If the child is two years old, you don't need to go into a detailed explanation. But as the child gets older and starts developing their own thinking capacity, then we need to say, "Here's what I want you to do because...." And give them a legitimate reason for following your particular request.

Here's a personal example. On the first Friday night after my son got his driver's license, he wanted to drive to West Texas, about 150 miles away, to a high school football game where his team was participating. I said to him, "Son, no you can't drive that far away. And the reason you can't is simply because on Friday nights there is a much higher percentage of drunks on the highway. Number two, the traffic is heavier because of all the high school football games. And your experience right now is not enough to deal with all of those situations. Your day is coming, but not now." There was no further discussion necessary. He said, "Okay."

When we give a reason for a decision, that's authoritative and that's what develops communication skills and trust and follow through. I'll never forget when a friend of mine and his family picked me up at the airport in Cleveland. We had agreed to go have lunch and then go on to the hotel where I was going to be staying. On the way, one of his sons who was about eight years old said that instead of going a certain way, his dad could take another route that would be faster.

My friend answered, "Well, son, I have thought about that, but as I thought it completely through, I realized that this was the more direct route because the lights are better arranged and organized. But that was a good idea you had. Thank you for bringing that to my attention." The father showed his son courtesy and respect. He listened to him. He was authoritative, not authoritarian. There's a huge difference. The authoritarians say, "Do it because I said so." The authoritative person says, "Here's the reason we do it." That makes for a much more cooperative spirit in the person.

> WHEN WE GIVE A REASON FOR A DECISION, THAT'S AUTHORITATIVE AND THAT'S WHAT DEVELOPS COMMUNICATION SKILLS AND TRUST AND FOLLOW THROUGH.

FINISHING WELL

In this final session you'll understand why we've covered everything in the previous chapters because now we're headed for the reason for doing all of that. Let's begin with this thought. When I discipline myself to eat properly, live morally, exercise regularly, grow mentally and spiritually, and not put any drugs or alcohol in my body, I have given myself the freedom to be at my very best, perform at my best, and reap all the rewards that go along with it—and that certainly includes finishing well.

When I think about finishing well, I think of my mentor Fred Smith and a phone call he received from his son, Fred Junior. He said to him, "Dad, why don't we go to London and look at some of the old bookstores and spend a considerable amount of time together." They agreed and they had an absolutely magnificent experience. Fred told me that the one thing that Fred Junior talked about and asked on every occasion was, "Dad, I know you've dealt with many executives over the years—men and women who've been tremendously successful in their lives. But, Dad, tell me, how did they finish. Did they finish well?"

That's a very important issue because it's certainly something all of us want to do—finish well.

As a youngster, one of my first assignments in the garden was to hoe two long rows of beans. There were two things I knew about my mother's assignments: First of all, I knew that she was going to show me exactly how to do it. Second, I knew that she was going to expect from me my very best. This is a very important point. She did not expect me or any of my brothers and sisters to

be the absolute best in the whole world at everything we did—
that would have been impossible. But she did expect us to do our
very best.

> # WHEN YOU DO YOUR BEST, IT SAVES YOU A LOT OF TIME BECAUSE YOU WON'T HAVE TO DO THE JOB OVER.

She always explained that when you do your best, it saves you
a lot of time because you won't have to do the job over. And more
importantly even than that, you can lie down at night with the
simple but effective feeling of knowing that you did your best.
You sleep better when you do that. When you do the best that
you can do, that's where the good feeling comes from and that
too will help you to finish well.

BORN A WINNER

In the game of life, we know that there are some people who
do a lot of wonderful, marvelous things, but for whatever reason
they're not in a position to receive much praise and recognition.

But the issue is your best performance. One of the things I want to emphasize is that you don't have to win them all in order to be a winner. For example, George Washington, as he fought for our country's freedom during the Revolutionary War, only won two battles—but those two were the most important battles, especially the last one. Abraham Lincoln was involved in fifteen elections and he only won three of them. But isn't he the man who really brought America to the realization that slavery was wrong, which led to freedom and the preservation of the Union itself?

You don't have to win them all to be a winner—but you have to give your best on every occasion to be the winner you were born to be and to enjoy a life that is absolutely magnificent. The commitment involved is absolutely tremendous, and well worth it.

I love the story of John Stephen Ahkwari who was a totally committed marathon runner in the 1968 Olympics in Mexico City. Early in the race he fell and severely injured his knee and ankle.

After a little medical attention where they bound up his bloody knee and ankle, he reentered the race to finish the marathon. He hobbled every step, each causing excruciating pain. When he finally crossed the finish line more than two hours after the last person who had finished before him, he actually took a victory lap.

When he finally came to a stop, the media asked him, "You knew you had absolutely no chance of winning the race, why didn't you just stop? You were hurt. You were in pain, yet you continued until you finished the race. Why?" John Stephen Ahkwari's answer should be an inspiration to you, as it still resonates in my mind. He said, "My country did not send me 7,000 miles to *enter* this race. They sent me 7,000 miles to *finish* the race." This happened many years ago yet people are still amazed at this story of commitment and persistence.

If you are in a position where you don't get a lot of praise and recognition, let me remind you that your objective is to finish the race, not just start the race. Regardless what anybody else says about you, your self-esteem, the commitment, the satisfaction, the joy that comes from giving it your best shot all of your life is absolutely beyond belief. That's one way you can rest assured that regardless of how much other people recognize you, you will have that internal satisfaction of knowing you did what was right, you gave it your best shot, and yes, you *will* finish well.

And your view from the top is going to be especially sweet!

> **YOUR OBJECTIVE IS TO FINISH THE RACE, NOT JUST START THE RACE.**

CHAPTER 11

ACTION STEPS
TO THE TOP

You're at the top when you stand in front of
the Creator of the universe and He says to you, "Well
done, good and faithful servant."

I 'm always amused when people proudly proclaim they are
self-made successes—that they did it all on their own. But
let's look at whether or not we really are self-made. Let me
repeat some information I have shared with you earlier. I have
twenty-six people on my wall of gratitude. You would not be reading this today had it not been for those people. Am I a self-made
man? Of course not. That's ridiculous. And you know what, I've
never met a really self-made person. I've met a lot who've overcome a tremendous number of obstacles and difficulties, but they
had help every step of the way—you can absolutely count on it.

When we talk about finishing well, our compassion for and interest in and concern for other people is of so much importance. I keep referring back to my own life and how my first-grade teacher knew the condition of our family and knew the importance of education.

So out of compassion in her heart, she came to our home while I was sick in bed for four months and she taught me two days a week to keep me caught up with my schoolwork. Her compassion made a huge difference in my life because I never would have finished high school had it not been for her. I would have been drafted out of high school. Finishing high school enabled me to get an education because I was able to get in the naval V5 program, which started in college.

Compassion is enormously important. Somebody said, "He climbs highest who reaches down and lifts another up." That's compassion. That's what's important. Faith is also important because *faith and fear cannot coexist.* As a matter of fact, it says in the Bible 365 times, "fear not." Fear is false evidence. If you want to form an acronym for FEAR: False Evidence Appearing Real. I'm talking about fear that's unreasonable. Obviously, you should be afraid to cross a busy stream of traffic coming and going both ways—that's common sense. But unrealistic fear is one of the greatest handicaps you will encounter.

So, this is where courage comes in. Courage is the base upon which everything else is built. If you don't have the courage to do what is right, to use what you need, to be willing to take those calculated risks, then you will not be nearly as successful or as happy in your life.

To tie all of these things together—compassion, faith, fear, and courage, I offer the following. Of the 1949 graduating class at Harvard University, which incidentally at that time did not permit women in the class, nearly 50 percent of them achieved tremendous success in their lives. They became at least vice presidents of major corporations or presidents and CEOs or chairmen of the board. A study was done on them, CNN did a 30-minute special on them, and a book was written about them. The question was asked of them, "Why do you feel that you've been so enormously successful?" Every man said the same thing. "First of all, everything we did was with integrity. Number two, we had wives who were not only bright but who were very supportive. They were full teammates with us; we worked together. And finally, we were risk takers but not gamblers."

There is a difference. And risk-taking involves a certain amount of courage particularly when you're in an executive position and everybody depends on the decisions you make to keep everything going. Where you stand determines where you sit—whether in a boardroom or classroom. If you have faith, courage, and compassion for others, then you function as a team member and you will finish well—because you have taken a lot of friends along with you. Put it all together and it spells success. Then you along with your friends and associates will enjoy the view from the top.

The final step when you arrive at your destination is not to only embrace what you have received by getting there—it is to recognize who you have become by reaching the destination that some people said you might never reach.

That final step includes expressing your gratitude and appreciation to all of the people who had a hand in your success and in your climb. Not only is it the right thing to do but it's a sign of class. *Gratitude is the healthiest of all human emotions.* When we wonderfully, freely express our gratitude, we are really displaying our true thankfulness for what others have done for us.

As I have mentioned, one of my favorite people and a friend of mine since his days at Arkansas is Lou Holtz. Lou gained an international reputation for writing personal thank-you notes to people from whom he received help and encouragement. It's a sign of class and I encourage you to write those notes and make those phone calls. You never know when those people to whom you're writing might be having a down day. They might be thinking their lives have not really meant very much to anyone, especially in recent days. Your note can be a tremendous motivational and uplifting boost.

Remember that you really can't have everything in life you want without helping other people get what they want. Everyone wants to be respected and appreciated and your note or phone call is expressing acceptance and expressing appreciation. Do it.

TWELVE STEPS

During the process of finishing well, I think the twelve steps from Alcoholics Anonymous really share with us a great deal of wonderful, wonderful advice. First of all, until you acknowledge you have a problem there's no way to solve it. That's the first step. Acknowledging doesn't always bring a solution—but until you acknowledge the problem, there's going to be no solution.

A lot of different organizations use these particular steps that work in a variety of circumstances. Whoever gets involved admits they have a problem, which is the first step to solving it.

Number two, they put their dependence on God as they understand Him. In other words, they recognize they have been working with that problem, struggling with it for years, and have been unable to solve it. They know they need help and so God, as they understand Him, is a major portion of the picture that focuses on solving the problem.

Another enormously important factor in the twelve steps refers to a biblical principle which says that in the counsel of the multitude there is wisdom. Friends and associates who have already overcome the problem give advice and provide companionship because loneliness is one of the reasons people have a drinking or drug problem.

Another principle that's exhilarating to me is the fact that we're admonished to get excited about problems and here's why. I have to admit I've never prayed and said, "Lord, give me a few more problems. I'm just having it too good." But maybe I should because problems produce patience, patience produces persistence, persistence produces character, character produces hope, and hope produces power. When you put all of these principles together that's what you find in the AA twelve-step program.

As long as a person has hope and as long as the person recognizes the power and as long as they recognize that something good can come out of their problem, then you don't ever want to overlook the good in a bad situation you've been in, because out of every situation that's bad, some good is there if we just look for it.

One of my favorite people in the whole world was Dr. Norman Vincent Peale. He came along in my own life at a very critical time—when I had my share of bad situations. In direct sales, field managers are directly responsible for the success of the organization. I had four field managers and each one failed—one right after the other. First of all, one who had been promoted in my place did not have the experience and his organization started to fall apart. Number two, one of them had an integrity problem and his organization collapsed. The third one had a heart attack and his organization collapsed. And the fourth had his big toe almost cut off and for twenty days he lay flat on his back, and for several months he was on crutches. His organization fell apart.

Then I had an organized, long-term pity party for myself—woe is me. I was being blamed for all of the difficulties and all I could think was, *It's not fair. I'm the good guy; they're the bad guys. I had nothing whatsoever to do with all of these problems.* Well, as you know, the basic problem with pity parties is that very few people come to them—and no one ever brings presents.

When walking down the street in Knoxville, Tennessee, I saw through the window of a bookstore a book on a shelf titled *The Power of Positive Thinking*. I thought to myself, *Boy, if I've ever needed a positive outlook, I need it right now!*

I bought the book and absolutely devoured it and Dr. Peale agreed with me. In that book, he said in so many words, Zig, it really isn't your fault about the fella having a heart attack, the fella having the integrity problem, the guy with the injured toe, and the one with the lack of experience. Those are really not your fault. But Zig, let me talk to you about *your* responsibility. You have a large organization and a lot of people depend on you for leadership. It's your policy. It's your conviction. It's your attitude that is going to make the difference in them. Now Zig, you know perfectly good and well that you can overcome all of these things—just use the experience you already have.

> ## PROBLEMS PRODUCE PATIENCE, PATIENCE PRODUCES PERSISTENCE, PERSISTENCE PRODUCES CHARACTER, CHARACTER PRODUCES HOPE, AND HOPE PRODUCES POWER.

I have to tell you, I was highly motivated after reading that book and out of sixty-six divisions, even though I had only inherited the job in April or May, we finished that year as fifth in the nation. It was a dramatic recovery. Why is this so important to me? Later in life, Dr. Peale became a very close friend of mine.

He and his wife and my wife and I toured Australia together. I had a chance to watch him under every circumstance imaginable. He not only was a brilliant man and a very prolific writer, he was also a team builder. He and his wife, Ruth, worked together as a team.

But Dr. Peale was one of the gentlest, most humble men I have ever known. I never saw him display any arrogance and never saw him be rude or unkind to anyone. As an example of his attitude, one time I met him in Australia, he came in from Singapore. He had flown all night long and at that point he was well over seventy years of age. When he saw me, he greeted me with a big, excited handshake and he said, "Zig, I gotta tell you what just happened. I was up all night on that airplane and I have to tell you what a young man said to me!" Dr. Peale proceeded to tell me a very exciting story about how he had been witnessing to a young man and the results he had achieved. Now let me simply say Dr. Peale spoke until after he was ninety years old. His zest for life, his enthusiasm, his encouraging word, but most of all his gentle humility carried him through.

Dr. Peale was wise, he was brilliantly educated, willing to help those in need of help, and he tried to encourage everyone he met. He certainly was a role model for me and he is on my wall of gratitude. His attitude, outlook on life, compassion, and commitment to others enabled him to thoroughly enjoy his view from the top because he surely made it there by taking a lot of people with him.

You can too with this type of attitude and commitment.

ACTION STEPS

At this point, there are some action steps that are absolutely critical to follow through on your way to the top.

Step number one: Make a list of all of the people who you are grateful to for having assisted you in your journey through life. That's a very important list. It will mean a lot to you and you need to let them know they have played a very important role in your life. It'll make *them* feel good. It will make *you* feel good. Ideally, you should place pictures of them on your wall of gratitude.

Step number two: Make a list of those people who have wronged you over a period of time and make absolutely certain you forgive them. I've talked about forgiveness quite a bit because it is extremely important. When you forgive people, it's astonishing how many times reconciliation follows because your forgiveness has cleared the air.

True story. At one stage in my life there were two people who did me wrong. I mean it was bad news. I sued both and the bottom line is the courts gave me everything I had sued for. Now in my mind that proved I had been right and they had been wrong. But I was dead wrong in one area; namely, I told a lot of people about those dirty dogs and what they had done to me. When I became a Christian on July 4, 1972, I realized that I needed to seek forgiveness. I was a little chicken about it; I didn't approach the two people right away. I even have to plead guilty to doing a little plotting about it.

On Christmas Day, I figured everybody would be in a forgiving mood, so that day I called each of the men and apologized for having entered the suit, explaining that we should have dealt with it as friends or associates. We should have dealt with it in an entirely different way. I apologized, asked for forgiveness, and both accepted my apology and said they had forgiven me. But interestingly enough, neither one acknowledged that they had been wrong in the deal, too. But that's not the important thing. I felt a tremendous amount of freedom as a result of asking them to forgive me.

But here's another interesting part of the story. I only talked with the one man over the next twenty-five years, but the other man and I renewed our business acquaintance and it's been very good, profitable for both of us. Forgiveness is absolutely, tremendously important as it removes a burden from your shoulders.

> FORGIVENESS IS ABSOLUTELY, TREMENDOUSLY IMPORTANT AS IT REMOVES A BURDEN FROM YOUR SHOULDERS.

If you cannot get in touch with the people on your list for whatever reason, you need to write them a letter. In that letter you need to accuse them of all the bad things they did. You need to list it out. You need to write something like, "This was a low-down, dirty trick you played on me. I can't believe you did it, etc." Write all that out—might be two pages, ten pages, twenty pages. Write everything that comes to mind.

And then once that letter is completely written, go out in the backyard with a book of matches and light a fire and burn each page one by one. As you burn each page, say, "You were wrong in doing this to me, but I now forgive you. I'm burning all evidence of it. It is going to be out of my mind forever." It's amazing what that will do for you. Do this only if you cannot get in touch personally with that person, or if it is a wrong that you do not want to get back involved with that person. For example, maybe it was an adulterous relationship and you don't want to get back in touch with the person to ask for forgiveness for your part because it may light the flame again. In that case, just write the letter, ask for forgiveness, and then burn that letter. It will definitely make a huge difference in your life and will certainly improve your view from the top.

IDENTIFYING THE TOP

When I wrote the manuscript for my book *Over the Top* and sent it to the publisher, they wrote back and said, "Zig, before you can tell people how to go *over* the top, you have to *identify* the top." So, I sat down to identify the top, figuring it would be a piece of cake. But I thought and I pondered quite a while. I did everything imaginable to try and identify the top. I took long walks, which always produces answers for me, but I could not come up with a viable explanation of what the top really is.

And then one day my wife and I went to Shreveport, Louisiana, to visit her sister in a nursing home. Many people in nursing homes are beyond human health. Many have Alzheimer's or other signs of dementia. Many of them have physical problems that are unbelievable. Fortunately, her sister is not nearly in that kind of shape. She does have multiple sclerosis and does need care, though. On this particular occasion, I watched my wife as she grabbed and hugged the people at the nursing home. They greet her warmly—even those with Alzheimer's somehow seemed to recognize her. She has a wonderful time hugging people.

Well, that particular day it was especially difficult for me to watch. I walked out of the room and went outside for a little walk. I started to pray and asked God to give me the same kind of heart, the same compassion for others that my wife had. I must have been gone for ten or fifteen minutes, and when I went back inside, everybody had moved into the great room where they had their meals and entertainment and parties. I sat down at the table with my wife and her sister, and all of a sudden, thoughts started to come into my mind.

The only piece of paper I had was the back of a motel bill, but I started to write. And in the next thirty minutes, 90 percent of what you're now about to read is what I wrote that day:

- You're at the top when you clearly understand that failure is an event, not a person.

- You're at the top when you realize that yesterday ended last night and today is your brand-new day.

- You're at the top when you made friends with your past, are focused on the present, and optimistic about your future.

- You're at the top when you know a win doesn't make you and failure doesn't break you.

- You're at the top when you're filled with faith, hope, and love and live without anger, greed, guilt, and the thoughts of revenge.

- You're at the top when you're mature enough to delay gratification and shift your focus from your rights to your responsibilities—when you know that failure to stand for what is morally right is a prelude to being the victim of what is criminally wrong.

- You're at the top when you're secure in who you are and are at peace with God and in fellowship with others.

- You're at the top when you made friends of your adversaries and have gained the love and respect of those who know you best.

- You're at the top when you understand that others can give you pleasure but genuine happiness comes when you do things for others.

- You're at the top when you're pleasant to the grouch, courteous to the rude, and generous to the needy.

- You're at the top when you love the unlovable, give hope to the hopeless, friendship to the friendless, and encouragement to the discouraged.

- You're at the top when you can look back in forgiveness, forward in hope, down in compassion, and up with gratitude.

- You're at the top when you know that whoever would be the greatest among you must become the servant of all.

- You're at the top when you recognize, confess, develop, and use your God-given physical, mental, and spiritual abilities to the glory of God and for the benefit of mankind.

- You're at the top when you stand in front of the Creator of the universe and He says to you, "Well done, good and faithful servant."

There is no question in my mind that when you seriously consider these fifteen points, make them part of your life, and use them on a daily basis, then you will truly have a magnificent view from the top.

ABOUT THE AUTHOR

ZIG ZIGLAR (1926–2012) was one of America's most influential and beloved encouragers and believers that everyone could be, do, and have more. He was a motivational speaker, teacher, and trainer who traveled extensively delivering messages of humor, hope, and encouragement. His appeal transcended age, culture, and occupation. From 1970 until 2010, Zig traveled more than five million miles around the world sharing powerful life-improvement messages, cultivating the energy of change.

Zig Ziglar wrote more than thirty celebrated books on personal growth, leadership, sales, faith, family, and success. He was a committed family man, dedicated patriot, and an active church member. His unique delivery style and powerful presentations earned him many honors, and today he is still considered one of the most versatile authorities on the science of human potential.